BOYS WILL BE ~~BOYS~~ HUMAN

A GET-REAL **GUT-CHECK** GUIDE TO BECOMING *the* **STRONGEST, KINDEST, BRAVEST** PERSON YOU can→ BE

JUSTIN BALDONI

HARPER

An Imprint of HarperCollinsPublishers

For Maxwell and Maiya, may you grow up in a world where boys are allowed to feel and be safe spaces not just for others, but for themselves; and where girls don't need protecting because they are not seen as objects but as people. And may you always remember that the strongest muscle in your body is your heart, that you are worthy and loved—and that you are and have always been enough.

Boys Will Be Human: A Get-Real Gut-Check Guide to Becoming
the Strongest, Kindest, Bravest Person You Can Be
Copyright © 2022 AFG Productions, Inc.
All rights reserved. Printed in the United States of America.
No part of this book may be used or reproduced in any manner whatsoever without written permission except in the case of brief quotations embodied in critical articles and reviews. For information address HarperCollins Children's Books, a division of HarperCollins Publishers, 195 Broadway, New York, NY 10007.
www.harpercollinschildrens.com

ISBN 978-0-06-306718-9

Typography by Corina Lupp

22 23 24 25 26 PC/LSCC 10 9 8 7 6 5 4 3 2 1

First Edition

CONTENTS

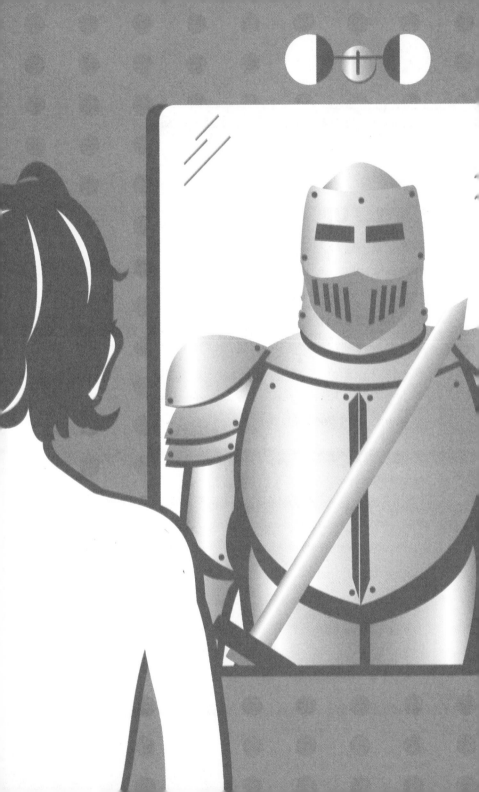

INTRODUCTION

HEADS UP! At times this book covers some mature topics. If you're younger than eleven, please make sure your parents or guardians are okay with you reading it. If you are eleven or older, just know that there could be some content you aren't quite ready to read or think about yet—that's okay! It's totally fine to skip sections or chapters and come back to them when you're ready. And if you are an adult reading this book to see if it's suitable for your child, be open: you may get just as much out of it as they will!

Hey! I'm Justin. Nice to meet you, my friend. Okay, well, obviously we're not *really* meeting, and we aren't really friends yet, but since you've chosen to pick up this book, I do hope it will feel like we are.

Since the most important thing in any friendship is trust, I should tell you a few things about myself. Trust is what every great and healthy relationship is built on, kind of like the foundation of a house. And the first step in building that foundation, that sense of trust, is sharing our stories and getting real with each other.

So, here is a little about me to get us started:

1. I'm an actor, probably best known for being on a TV show called *Jane the Virgin*. I'm a director (*Five Feet Apart* and *Clouds* are two of the movies I've made) and I started a movie studio called Wayfarer Studios, where we aspire to make movies and TV that help us remember that we are human and that we are all far more alike than we are different. I also do a bunch of other things for work, and I'd like to think I am way more than my career accomplishments (even though that's what the world places the most value on).

2. I LOVE food. Honestly, if I wasn't an actor or director, I think I would want to be a chef. What I love even more than making food is eating it! Pizza, pasta, sushi, BBQ, tacos . . . you name it. And my favorite part about any food is the sauce that goes on that food. I'm obsessed with sauces. I think my restaurant would probably be called Sauce.

3. I also love sports (I was a soccer player growing up),

traveling, reading, working out, and biohacking (you probably have no idea what that is, but that's okay; you won't need to for another twenty years).

4. I'm a dad to my two incredible and wild kids, Maiya and Maxwell, and a husband to my amazing wife Emily, who I am madly in love with. I would do anything for them. They are my everything.

5. I wrote this book for boys and anyone who loves them, but don't worry, this is not a *boy hating, we must apologize for being born* type of book. In fact, it's the opposite! It's a *boy loving, we have the power to change the world* book. However, if I say something that you don't really agree with, I ask you to keep reading, because I believe with all my heart that when we don't agree, we can still learn from each other. That's actually how we find the truth—through listening to differing opinions and points of view.

6. I'm Bahá'í (that's my faith), but this is not a Bahá'í book by any means, and I don't speak for the Bahá'í community. If you've never heard of it, that's okay. You aren't alone. Basically, in a nutshell Bahá'ís believe in the unity of all religions, like all the religions are different chapters in one book. The Bahá'í faith teaches that every human on the planet is important,

and that part of our mission here on earth is to set our differences aside and realize that we are all one human family. My faith has always been a lighthouse in the darkness for me, guiding me and helping me remember that each of us can change the world through acts of service, love, and compassion. You'll hear me talk about my faith here and there throughout the book because it has shaped my view of the world and inspired me in my work, but please know that whatever your beliefs are, I respect them even though they might be different from mine.

Okay! Now that we have gotten the get-to-know-me part out of the way, you may have noticed one of the things I didn't list was being an author. That's because I'm still getting used to it. See, when I was growing up, I never thought I was smart enough or good enough to become a writer, and books were kind of intimidating to me. They reminded me of school, and school was not always my happy place. But I am going to own it now because you are reading this book, which means I did it! I am an author. *Author.* (I'm saying it with a fake British accent right now, and it sounds even better.)

Now that you know a little more about me, I'm going to

confess something—this book isn't really about me . . . it's about *you* and what it might be like to be you, right now, this very minute.

WAIT, THIS BOOK IS ABOUT *ME?*

Yep. Well, *us*, actually. Boys. Men. Male humans. You get the picture.

More important, this book is about our questions. The big ones we think about but never say out loud. The ones about becoming and eventually being a man. The ones that can help us not just grow up to be better men, but better humans. It's also about what it means to be *enough* in every sense of the word.

This book raises questions about masculinity and looks closely at how the answers to these questions shape who we are. Some of the questions are about our bodies; some are about our minds. Some questions are about things that make us uncomfortable or afraid (yes, men can absolutely be afraid). Some of them are about things that will not only make us stronger but happier, too. All of them are about things that make us human.

As for the answers to these questions, well . . . honestly,

I'm still trying to figure them out. In fact, this all started as an adult book called *Man Enough: Undefining My Masculinity*, which is based on a TED Talk I did and has also become a podcast. I wrote it as a way to understand how I feel about manhood and the challenges I've faced trying to live up to other people's expectations of me. See, I love being a man, but that doesn't mean I know exactly how to become the kind of man I want to be, or that I don't question how the world tells me I should act as a man. Also, even though I'm now in my thirties, my thoughts and opinions about the world and myself change every day. That's why I wrote this book: not as your teacher or an expert on the subject, but as a friend, a fellow student, and as a work in progress, which is what every single human being on this planet is.

No one is perfect. No one has it all figured out (even though social media can make it seem like some do). But all of us are doing our best. So, this is me doing my best to share what I've learned on my own journey in hopes that if you're feeling anything like I did growing up—confused, worried, anxious, like I didn't measure up, even a little afraid—then maybe you can see yourself in these words and remember that you aren't the only one feeling that way. If anything, I want this book to feel like a trusted friend to you whenever you need a reminder that you are good, worthy, and more than enough.

There are a lot of misconceptions about what masculinity is. Lately in the news or media it seems to be talked about as a bad thing, which it's not. Masculinity is basically the traits, characteristics, and qualities that men or boys have, or are believed or assumed to have. Also, I just want to say that I believe that boys and men are good: inherently, intrinsically good. That YOU are good. And there are tons of aspects of the traditional definition of masculinity that I'm grateful for and agree with! I'm 100 percent not ashamed to say I love being a man. There are so many positive traits and qualities that have been associated with masculinity and being a man that I aspire to embody and live by—traits like being resourceful and accountable, honest and trustworthy, hardworking, loyal, and a present father and husband. But the question then becomes—are these qualities reserved just for boys, or are they for everyone?

For instance, if I asked a random person to name some masculine qualities, they might say things like "strong, hardworking, brave, powerful, focused, competitive, tough." And if I asked the same person to name some feminine qualities, they might say other things, like "caring, gentle, emotional, sensitive, nurturing, attentive, feeling, and kind." But why is there this line drawn in the sand? And is drawing this line helping any of us?

Think of it this way: if we were developing a state-of-the-art robot that was going to take over the world and accomplish all our tasks—do all the things that need to get done—we'd want it to have all the masculine qualities you could think of. But if we wanted to make that robot a human and bring it to life . . . we would give it all the feminine qualities, right?

Too often the messages of masculinity turn us boys and men (myself included) into robots. Which is why it's so important to me that we undefine masculinity and embrace ALL the qualities that make us human.

SO WHAT EXACTLY DOES "UNDEFINING MASCULINITY" EVEN MEAN? SOUNDS COMPLICATED.

For me, "undefining masculinity" means questioning the rules of how boys are supposed to behave. I mean, who actually makes or decides these rules anyway? Who gets to say what it means to be a boy or a man today? Is there some secret meeting that happens where our masculinity is judged and where a group of elders in cloaks get together in the middle of the night and decide who makes the cut? No. There are no real rules, just messages that have been passed down from generation to generation but are never really talked about.

These messages and unspoken rules don't just show up in our family. They are EVERYWHERE. While many of those messages are good and universal to both boys and girls (like being honorable, honest, living with integrity, and standing up for what's right), many of them actually hurt us more than help us. Here's the one that I believe hurts us the most: "real" boys (as if there is such a thing as "*not* real" boys) don't show anyone how we feel or talk about our feelings. Oh, and we definitely don't *cry* (unless we lose a big game—for some reason ONLY then is it okay). There are other harmful ones, too: Boys don't ask for help or admit when we're wrong. We have no insecurities and never back down from a fight. We pledge allegiance to the other boys even if they aren't our friends, and we understand that a man should be strong— not just in his body but in his mind—and not let anything bother us. **ANYTHING.** Therefore, we must always wear an invisible suit of armor, so that we're impervious to all the negative things the world can throw at us.

But armor is *heavy*. It's uncomfortable. It not only keeps things out, but it also keeps us locked in.

I've lugged my armor around my whole life, and not only has it kept me from experiencing my own emotions, it also stopped me from truly connecting with my friends, parents, coworkers, kids, and even my wife. So now I'm taking that armor off, piece by piece. And real talk? I've never felt better, freer, or more like the real me.

My only regret was that it took me so long to rip it off. I just wish I could travel back in time and have someone give me this book and tell me not to put that armor on when I was a kid. That it was going to end up hurting me and the people I cared about so much more than it would ever help me. That's another reason why I wrote this book: to tell you the things I wish someone had told me when I was growing up.

"Undefining masculinity" also means not judging people based on a binary system, which is loosely defined as something with two distinct parts. In this case, it's *masculine* and *feminine*, and many of us have been taught to believe that boys and girls are opposites. We're not. Sure, science tells us very clearly that men and women have biological differences, but those differences are things that should be celebrated, valued, and appreciated and not used to separate us or pit us against each other. Equality doesn't mean we are all the same. It just means we are all treated the same and no one is punished or treated as "less than" for being different.

Undefining masculinity is basically making room for you, as a boy and eventually as a man, to not have to be a robot that must act a certain way, talk a certain way, feel or not feel a certain way, do a bunch of work, or complete a bunch of tasks so that you can take over the world. Instead, undefining masculinity is a way for you (and for me) to stop being robots and start being humans. Because as humans, we have all those qualities in us. As humans we are strong because we are kind, brave because we are vulnerable, and cool because we care. We all have feelings. We're all just trying to be our best selves. We're all just human. Which is why I believe we need to undefine masculinity to make space for ANYONE who sees themselves as a boy or a man to be treated like one. And how should boys treat other boys (and really all other humans)? With compassion and acceptance, even if they look or act different than you.

Yep, it's that simple. Undefining masculinity is basically just creating more room for yourself to become a full and kind human.

OKAY, BUT WHY SHOULD I READ THIS BOOK?

All right, hear me out. Imagine if there was a holiday where we could all *tell the truth*. For one day a year, everyone could officially let their guard down and say what they actually think and feel—no matter how complicated or strange. The only rule would be that no one could judge us. There would be no risk of being ridiculed or made fun of. We would all be completely free to mean what we say and say what we mean.

Does the idea of a day like that kind of freak you out? Me too! It *shakes* me. If I admitted that I was scared, or confused, or totally unsure of everything, people might see me as flawed. Worst of all, other men might see the crack in my armor, and then they might think I was weak. According to the unspoken rules of manhood, one exposed weak spot and you are vulnerable to attack.

I don't know about you, but I think it's about time we all stop worrying about being perfect and start being real. My hope is that reading this book will help you be more honest with yourself and comfortable with who you are, no matter what other people think.

Also, as you read this book, just know that you're in for

an honest conversation that will bust the "boys will be boys" myth wide open and demand that we stop making excuses for the ways in which our behavior hurts each other and those around us.

So, what's the myth? Well, it's the belief that boys and men will behave a certain way—wild, violent, insensitive, unfeeling—because it's in our nature. And how can you deny something in a creature's nature? You can't blame us for how we act, because it's hardwired into our DNA.

But science shows that the opposite is true. In 2014, University of California, Berkeley's education director Vicki Zakrzewski's research found that boys were just as emotionally aware and sensitive as girls—they just had no space to address their feelings: "cultivating their natural capacity for emotional attunement and relationships is critical to [boys'] overall well-being," she wrote. "But we can't wait till they're men to do so—we need to start when they're young."

Luckily, you're young!

Take me for instance. I was a pretty emotional, sensitive boy wrapped inside a testosterone tornado. Since I couldn't sit still most of the time, sports became my outlet, but my emotions weren't welcome on the team. Even though I was super athletic, my sensitivity stuck out and I was picked on and bullied because I was an easy target. So I built up my armor to make sure no one could see that my feelings were hurt—and even worse, I picked on other kids and hurt their feelings to make myself feel better.

Only years later did I realize that I was *performing* the unwritten script of masculinity. It was all an act. And everyone—male friends and teachers, fathers and even famous movie stars—were playing the same role. We were taking part in a vicious cycle that was actively chipping away at our minds, hearts, and, most important, our souls.

Look, I'm not a professor, or a psychologist, or a guidance counselor—but I hope I feel like someone you can trust, because I promise you that I will always tell you the truth. It might be messy and uncomfortable at times (especially if you are reading this with your parents), but it will be worth it.

I just want to make this clear, too: while you and I may share a lot of the same experiences with masculinity, it's important to note that I'm white and heterosexual, which means that some of my lived experience may be different from yours. Also, throughout this book, when I say "boys," "guys," or "men" (or any other form of the gender), I am including anyone and everyone who identifies themselves as a man, and when I say "we" or "us" I am including myself in that group.)

That said, I do believe that the unwritten rules of masculinity affect us all in very similar ways. As an example, one of my favorite reviews of my adult book *Man Enough* came from a friend of mine who happens to be an older, Black trans man. I honestly never thought that he and I would have had similar experiences, and I was a bit nervous for him to read my book. But when he messaged me after reading about my journey and told me that he had tears streaming down his face because it was one of the first times he felt truly seen as a man, I realized that these unwritten rules, as harmful as they can be, actually unite us more than we realize. So as you are reading there might be times when you don't relate to some of my personal stories or points of view—that's totally okay! Just know I have compassion for everything you are feeling and trying to figure out, and hopefully reading about an experience different from yours can help you too!

Oh, and one more important thing to remember: I *love* being a man, but I believe wholeheartedly that above all we are spiritual beings having and sharing a physical experience. That means regardless of our gender, what's important to our spiritual growth is learning how to be kind, loving, honest, of service, thoughtful, sensitive, loyal, steadfast, compassionate, and humble (and that's just to name a few). But this world can be scary and full of tests and trials meant to distract us from taking this journey from our heads to our hearts, and oftentimes those qualities I listed are not rewarded as much as others. In the face of that, though, I hope we can all rise to the occasion and show up as our best, most authentic selves. For me that looks like not just trying to be the best man I can be, but the best human I can be.

ALL RIGHT, LET'S DO THIS. NOW WHAT?

The next step is taking a deep breath and diving in.

But I have one last thing to tell you before you do.

When you read this book, you're going to have to think with your gut, not with your head. If that's new to you, then imagine thinking with your body, not with your brain. Some call it intuition, others call it a gut feeling, but regardless of what we call it, one thing I have learned is that our bodies are incredible, intelligent, sensitive things that feel so much more than we realize.

But listening to our bodies isn't easy, because as boys we are taught that our bodies are only for things like sports, play, sex, or fighting, when in reality our bodies hold our souls and are our first true friends. And like any good friendship, it requires trust and the ability to be listened to.

I know a lot of people say things like "Listen to your heart" or "Your heart will guide you." I appreciate that idea, but it's much easier said than done. It's taken me years and years to learn how to listen to my heart and feel into my body, and even now at my age I still don't always listen. See, my heart is *so* full of emotions—fear, love, resentment, joy, rage, envy, confusion—that it's hard to listen to it without getting caught up in all my feelings. But my brain is no good either, because it sees my feelings as a threat and tries to rationalize them, focusing only on my goal, or on information.

Your body has that core understanding of what's right and what's wrong. Your gut reacts whether you want it to or not, and no matter how much you think or feel about something, the true answer that hits you in your body never really changes. But acting on your gut feelings and doing the right thing isn't automatic.

It's a choice you make.

So how do you feel? You ready?! Me neither, but that's okay.

We're going to do this together.

1

BOYS WILL BE
BRAVE

LEAP OF FAITH

"Come on, Boner, don't be a girl!"

I'll never forget hearing my friend Tim say that. There I was, twelve years old, shivering as I looked over the edge of the bridge. He and a few other guys waded in the river twenty feet below me, waiting for me to jump in after them. The water seemed fine—no whitewater rapids, no sharks' fins circling beneath me. All it would take was a quick leap over the guardrail and the balls to jump into the water.

He might as well have been asking me to jump off the Empire State Building.

What was I going to do, tell them the truth? That I was terrified of heights if there wasn't a rail or window to keep me safe? That I had tried to jump already—really, I had, ten different times—but that my body wouldn't budge?

Nope. Not an option. My choices were either "man up" and jump, or refuse—and be called a girl.

So I jumped. Not because I wanted to, or because I enjoyed it, but because I'd rather break my neck than be a girl. Because we all know what being called a girl really means, right? It means we are weak, which is funny, because I know a few girls who would've jumped off that bridge way quicker than any of us. In the minds of us twelve-year-old boys, being called a girl was the worst thing we could be for some reason, and having my masculinity stripped away from me felt like the worst thing, too.

Looking back, I remember something my mom used to say. When I wanted to go do whatever stupid thing all the other boys in my class were doing, she'd say, "If everyone else jumped off a bridge, would you?" What she was trying to say was, "Don't do something dumb just because everyone else does it."

When faced with being labeled a girl I *literally jumped off a bridge.*

What does that say about the way I was being taught to view girls? That they were less than me? That I'd rather hurt myself than be seen as one?

Technically, the teasing worked. When I hit the water, I didn't die. When I rose to the surface, Tim and my other friends shouted, "Yeah, Boner!" (The stupid nickname my friends made up started as "Balboner," a play on my last name, Baldoni. Good one, right? They weren't exactly Shakespeare.) The guys cheered for about five seconds, and then we went swimming. I'd faced my fear, and I'd won. And the worst part was that I felt amazing for winning.

Only I hadn't actually won—I'd lost, big time. I'd done something I didn't want to because I was scared of what the other guys would think of me. I'd let fear shove me off that bridge, and I ignored everything my body was telling me in the process. And yet I have to admit that I still felt amazing.

Did I feel amazing because I pushed past my comfort zone and past my limits and fear? Not really. I felt amazing because of the acceptance and validation I got from the other boys, mixed with the adrenaline rush of jumping off something high and NOT dying. When that feeling wore off, I was still afraid, but now that I had jumped once, there was no way I could ever show my fear again.

THE SECRET LANGUAGE OF MALE BRAVERY

It might seem like the lesson I learned that day was that being a boy means being able to silence that voice in my body that's telling me I'm afraid and pushing through my fears, but is that really the lesson? Is that what's actually best for me, or just what will keep me from being made fun of or called a name? And was my fear of being called a girl even justified? Let's dig in.

What can be so confusing about being a boy, especially when we're in a group, is that we think that what makes us cool or strong is our ability to quiet those voices and take physical risk. It's almost like the more dangerous the thing we are being pressured to do is, the cooler we are, but that's actually false. Sure, we might get some temporary props or go viral for doing something cool, but eventually we will have to one up it, so is it really worth it?

The way I see it, the more we teach ourselves to ignore a part of our body that is trying to tell us something, the more we sever that connection between our head and our heart. We stop ourselves from feeling not just fear, but all sorts of emotions. Emotions that we will need the rest of our lives to be able to be happy and healthy.

Now, let's unpack the language that pushed me off the bridge. We can all admit that on a scale of "jerk" to the F-bomb, being called a girl is not usually seen as a very serious insult. What scared me is what being called a girl represented. Because what my friends were actually saying was that I wasn't *really* one of the boys because I wasn't brave enough.

But what we don't often think about is that if we examine why we feel attacked or threatened when someone calls us a girl, we may find that we have bought into the idea that we don't value girls as much as we value ourselves. If we view someone as less than us, how will we ever truly respect them or see them as equal?

Our language matters, and even though a part of you might cringe if you're called a girl or soft, what we really need to do is push through THAT feeling. Someone else's gender—or sexual orientation—should never be used an insult. Besides, it only feels insulting to us if we 1) let it and 2) think less of who we're being compared to. And as boys that's the last thing we should be thinking.

Now I know this doesn't change how it feels to be seen as "soft" or "wimpy." It hurts, and we want to do whatever we can to avoid that hurt at all costs. For me it felt like a death sentence of sorts, but we have to ask ourselves the question of what's worse: not living up to someone else's or society's expectation of us, or not living up to our own expectation of ourselves?

On that day at the bridge, I decided I'd rather give in and do the thing that scared me the most instead of letting them call me a girl. I chose them over me. And this is something I would continue to do for years.

Though I wasn't aware of it at the time, jumping off the bridge taught me two things: First, that being a boy wasn't about what you wanted to do or how you felt, but about *what other boys told you to do and how you should feel*. And second, that being brave in the eyes of other boys was more important than anything else in the world—including listening to my gut.

These lessons would stay with me for most of my life. Neither of them ever did me any good. More important, they were the opposite of what I knew in my heart to be true—*that being brave is about doing what you know is right*. But "right" is going to look different to each of us, because even though we all might be boys, we don't all come from the same background and experience.

Still, "brave" is a word that comes up a lot when people try to lock down what it takes to be a man. "Real" men

GUT CHECK

RETHINKING BRAVERY

Grab a sheet of paper and write down a list of things you consider brave that other boys might think aren't necessarily "manly." You can use my story as an example. I think it would have been brave to tell my friends that I wasn't jumping and honor my fears. Another act of bravery could be jumping off the bridge on my own terms and earning the amazing feeling from overcoming my fear. Another example could be stopping another boy from teasing someone, or even asking for help when you don't know the answer. From that list, pick something that you'd be scared to do that isn't seen as "typically" masculine, and think about why.

shouldn't be afraid of anything, much less a seemingly harmless twenty-foot jump. But maybe it's time we looked at what bravery really means, and where our definition of "brave" got a little turned around.

Somewhere along the way, as boys we get trained to think the wrong things are brave. We get convinced that bravery means being so fearless that we don't show our emotions at all. That a truly brave man not only ignores how he feels, but he also *stops* himself from feeling emotions so that he can do what's right. Feelings? That's girl stuff.

This idea is sad for a lot of reasons, and one of them is that this is so unfair to girls. It creates this invisible barrier, where girls are on one side and boys are on the other and we're told we can't understand each other. This barrier totally ignores that girls and women are just human, too, no better or worse than boys. These ideas of masculinity don't just hurt us, they hurt people we love.

And they definitely hurt. More and more, I've come to realize that it takes *so much effort* to not feel things, or not let anyone around you know what you're feeling (because let's face it, the feelings come whether you want them or not). Smiling when you're sad takes a lot of energy, and so does hiding how much you care about someone. Best-case scenario, you're wearing this thick metal armor in public all the time and sneaking off to feel all your feelings privately and enjoy the things and people that actually make you happy.

Think about that: that's the best-case scenario. Hiding who you really are.

So what should you do if you are ever in a situation like I was that day? You might think my answer is going to be "Never jump off that bridge!"

But it's not. Because sometimes, it's important to jump off that bridge. Not when everyone's calling you a wimp, or when you're being pressured to do so. But when *you* want to, *because* you want to. Doing things that challenge us or feel scary is a really important part of being human. We should all be allowed to take that leap, but that leap should happen when we're ready, on our own terms. And the only way we can know when we're ready is by quieting all the noise and listening to our bodies.

MALE INFLUENCERS: OUR SILENT TEACHERS OF MASCULINITY

When I say "influencer," I don't mean someone with a lot of followers on social media. I'm talking about the other boys and men in your life who influence the way you think and act every day without even realizing it.

For the record, this isn't just about men and boys—it's about everyone. All this is based on an idea called "socialization," which means that the ways we interact with people every day impact how we live and who we are. This can be schools, workplaces, family situations, sports teams, even the playground. Every day we are absorbing hundreds of spoken

GUT CHECK

AN EMBARRASSING MOMENT

Think about a time that you were red-faced embarrassed. What about it embarrassed you? In retrospect, was it actually funny? Would you have laughed if it happened to someone else? Are you still mortified about it? As you think about what happened, what does it feel like in your body? Do you think you can let this feeling of embarrassment go now, or is there more work to do there? Either way, see if you can close your eyes and feel what you maybe didn't allow yourself to feel the day it happened. Then take a deep breath, give it a sound, and shake it out and let it go!

and unspoken messages without even realizing it . . . and it's a lot to take in.

The thing about socialization is it's not usually intentional. These people who are influencing you—sometimes in negative ways—probably aren't doing it on purpose. Usually, they're holding you to a standard that they themselves were taught without ever really knowing it. The men in our lives aren't handing us a written set of rules when we're born and demanding we follow them, but they are over time telling us what is acceptable behavior by demonstrating it and punishing us or shaming us when we break free of the rules.

And the most confusing part is that it isn't JUST men who influence us; it's women, too. When we are all raised in the same culture, everyone is socialized to believe the same things. But who wrote the rules in the first place?! That's the thing about masculinity—even those who enforce the rules don't realize that they themselves have been performing and following a script that they didn't write and has been passed down to them.

So just know in the following section when we list these influencers, we're not trying to blame certain people in our lives or make them the "bad guy." It's just important to remember that there is a very good chance that groups of these people might influence us. Again, we're all in this together.

Since "socialization" might be a new word for you, I'll give you an example of it: in seventh and eighth grade, I loved being in drama class and acting in school plays. I got to play fun roles, like both Mercutio and Paris in *Romeo and Juliet*, where I could be quirky and weird (I also got to die twice). In middle school, we were allowed to both perform in the play *and* play a sport—in fact, it was encouraged. But as I got ready for high school, I quickly realized that

I couldn't do both. If I wanted to act in the fall play, I'd have to give up soccer; if I did the spring play, track and field were out. I had been playing soccer my whole life and always thought it would be my ticket to college, but acting made me really happy. I wasn't sure which one I'd choose, sports or theater . . . until my first day of freshman year, one of the most terrifying days of my life.

High school was so intimidating to me. In middle school, I would hear all these rumors and stories about the things that happen in high school. I would look at all the older boys—scratch that, older *guys* and their muscles and facial hair—and feel so small and like I would never measure up. The girls all seemed to be interested in the athletes. The ones who sat at the top of the food chain. And the theater kids? Well, at my school they got called weird and had 7-Eleven Slurpees tossed at them at lunch.

So without even putting much thought into it, I picked sports, and even though it hurt to give up acting, I didn't allow myself the chance to feel it or grieve the loss because I was too busy just trying to fit in. What's wild is that no one had ever actually made fun of me for doing theater in middle school or for wanting to do it in high school. No one told me what to do or what not to do—but I picked up messages from the people around me and internalized them. I made my decision out of fear and the desire to maybe one day be popular and at the top of the food chain. What I basically said to myself was, "Sports are for 'real' men." And I wanted to be a real man.

> ## "THE **STRONGER** A MAN IS, THE MORE **GENTLE** HE CAN AFFORD TO BE."
> ### ELBERT HUBBARD
> #### AMERICAN WRITER AND PHILOSOPHER

INFLUENCER GROUP 1: FAMILY

This is probably the group of influencers who have the most sway over your life, and who are the hardest to ignore. When our families influence our masculinity, the issue is that it usually comes from a place of love and protection. They want you to behave in a certain way because they want you to have what they perceive to be a good life and to take the path of least resistance: meaning they don't want you to do something that could make your life harder or put you in situations that could get you hurt physically or emotionally. And as we've said already, there's a good chance that the older men in our lives, whether they are our fathers, brothers, uncles, or cousins, have probably never even talked about these ideas. They have just spent their lives following the rules without ever even realizing it.

They probably never had a book like this, and that's not their fault.

For those us of who have dads or stepdads, the relationships can often be really complicated. For many of us, our fathers are our direct models for how men should act and how brave and tough men should be. And while many dads out there end up raising their sons to be like them, it's important to remember that our dads were also influenced and molded by their dads before them, not to mention the process of becoming a dad.

When you think about it, it's kind of like playing that game of telephone we all played when we were younger. You know the game, when one person starts and whispers a sentence in someone's ear and by the time it goes through five or six kids, the sentence is totally different? It's kind of like that, except with every generation, as the world changes, we change the script a little bit, but not nearly enough.

Now imagine a billion different games of telephone all happening at the same time, and each game has the same sentence but said a little differently. By the time the sentence has reached you or me, it's almost unrecognizable from how it started. The results of that are billions of men around the world being raised with old ideas of what it means to be a man in a modern and changing world—a world where labels and definitions are not helping us but instead are hurting us. But the good news is that each generation gets a little better than the one before, and together we get to write a new script.

My grandpa lived during a time when what it meant to be a man to him was pretty different than what it means to be a man today. Yet so much of what I learned growing up about manhood comes from him because he taught my dad, and my dad taught me!

My grandfather, a state senator, came to America from Italy in 1912 when he was eight, landing on Ellis Island with his brother, sister, and mom. During this time in America, Italian immigrants were experiencing widespread discrimination, prejudice, and even violence. Because of this, my grandfather grew up under the pressures of feeling like he had a lot to prove to the people around him. He was hard-working, well-spoken, and confident.

But the traditional scripts of what it meant to be a man back then manifested in how he parented my dad and his other children. My grandfather worked hard to provide for his family, and as a result, he was barely ever home.

It won't come as much of a surprise to hear that my grandfather wanted my dad and his siblings to assimilate and grow up as Americans, not as Italian immigrants. He didn't want them to face the same discrimination and stereotypes that he had. He was also a proud man, and he felt that image was important, especially as an immigrant living the American Dream.

Part of protecting that image was that he couldn't disclose our family's struggles (aka his humanity) because the family had to be seen a certain way to be accepted (or in his case, to be reelected). But it wasn't just a message my grandfather was sending to his children; it was a message that he had learned, and one that he would hold himself to until he passed away.

It actually took me writing the adult version of this book to get my dad to open up to me about his dad. And then after it came out, we decided to do an episode of the *Man Enough* podcast together where we went even deeper. It was an amazing and super emotional experience for both of us. Turns out, as wonderful a man as my grandfather was, he had a lot of room to improve as a father. Like the fact that he never went to any of my dad's football games in middle school or wrestling matches in high school. Or that despite adoring him, he never once told my dad those three words every kid needs and deserves to hear from their parents: "I love you."

What's important to remember here is that even fathers who are tough on their sons and teach them the ideas of "boys don't cry" or tease them for "throwing like a girl" don't do it because they are mean or want to cause trauma. I believe they genuinely just want to raise a boy who's going to be ready for the harsh world out there, a world that will walk all over a boy who shows weakness.

You see, if you have a dad, before he was your dad, he was a boy. He went to school, scraped his knee; at some point he drew a turkey by tracing his hand on a sheet of paper, and more than likely even had his own awkward moments with his erections during puberty (we'll talk more about this later). He probably worried about a lot of the things we'll talk about in this book—and in fact, he might have worried about them even more, because he was born before books like this were being written for boys. When he was a boy, boys were raised (even more than now) to be strong and independent and figure out everything on their own. For him, the rules of masculinity were driven home even harder by influencers, and the media, not to mention wars and other massive world events.

Understanding and having compassion for our dads, the father figures, mentors, and role models in our lives, means knowing that they can also feel hurt, and that it's okay for them to hurt. With that in mind, we can understand how seeing us go through our own pain—from worrying about our bodies to worrying we'll never be loved—can hurt our dads' hearts again. Even if they don't show us their pain. Remember, just like us, our dads were taught to swallow their emotions. They were taught that expressing their true feelings made them look weak. And the way socialization works (as weird as it is), your dad might actually feel that he can't admit or show his feelings to you because you're another boy and he has to lead by example to protect you.

Part of leading is not showing emotion. What if you see him as weak? What if you find out he actually has fears? In his mind, he might think showing his son that he doesn't have all the answers will make him a bad father. But that kind of honesty would benefit you more than almost anything else he could do.

You might not believe this, but every adult man in your life, including your dad, when he was young, was still dealing with a lot of the same insecurities as you. He may never admit it, but he still had a lot of wounds with armor on them instead of bandages, and he had a lot of questions that went unanswered. I know this because I'm a grown man and a dad, and it wasn't until AFTER I had kids that I felt like my wounds had started healing. But they weren't going to heal themselves . . . I had to do it.

Based on what I've told you so far about my life, you might think that my dad is a big, tough guy, but he's actually the opposite. My dad is one of the most genuine, kind, sweet, and sensitive men I have ever met, and I feel so lucky that he is my dad. But even though *he* didn't influence me to take on more of the old-school scripts of masculinity like many of my friends' dads, the world sure did. And then the world influenced me to feel ways about him.

When I was a kid, I *wanted* my dad to be more "manly." I wanted him to be a rugged, emotionless, no-nonsense guy, because when my family moved to a rural part of Oregon when I was a kid, those were the dads I saw around us. Isn't it interesting? Even when it isn't *our* fathers who are influencing us, the images we have of other fathers affects the way we see the world. So even though my dad was a successful businessman who was emotional and thoughtful and always showed up for me, because he didn't work with his hands, or teach me how to hunt or fight, or take me camping, I saw him as weak.

While every family looks different, I think it's important to point out that there's a good chance that one or more of these influencers may not apply to you. But that's okay; just because you may not have a father or a brother doesn't mean that you won't have a someone in your life who will influence you in a similar way. As an example, I don't have a brother, but I have been influenced by plenty of my friends' brothers. When they're older than you, brothers can give both helpful and terrible advice and also take out their own frustrations on their little siblings. When they're younger than you, brothers can seem like an embodiment of everything you don't like about yourself—the "little baby" you're trying not to be, or the annoying kid who tags along and repeats everything you say and do.

What's important to remember about brothers is that most of the time, whether they're younger or older, they're just as afraid as you, but just like you they aren't allowed to show it (especially not to someone who may be younger or smaller than them). When they're being unhealthy influencers—peer pressuring, introducing their siblings to adult things too early (like porn or even drugs), or making fun of their siblings—older brothers are often trying to overcome their own insecurities and process their own feelings. They're trying to show that *they're* not afraid by being tough to someone who will always look up to them.

There are also the extended family influencers—uncles, cousins, grandfathers. These influencers can be especially tricky to deal with because they don't have the day-to-day responsibility of being a part of the family, so they can feel like alternative sources of information about life or the world. *Your dad and brother and teachers and friends may tell you this, but let me tell you something, kid . . .*

But for a lot of boys, these family members aren't always

HEADS UP! Congrats! You're halfway through the first chapter. Little wins are important to celebrate and this is a win! Also, sometimes short breaks help me retain the information I just read, so if you need to, set this aside for a few minutes and start again later. Otherwise, let's keep at it.

around and maybe don't have a complete understanding of who we are as people. In their minds, how you behaved at your last birthday, when surrounded by other people and jacked up on sugar, is an example of everything they need to know about you. Or maybe they think they know you through social media. Regardless, it's easy to see extended-family influencers as giving you "real talk," or passing down the cheat codes for life, but these men are just men—just human—like the rest of us.

I also think it's important to remember that most family members love you dearly, and a lot of the time, their advice just comes from a place of wanting to help. But while their intention might be good, the impact it can have can actually be harmful and get in the way of your own growth. These influencers can become critical voices in your head that you can use to convince yourself you need to act a certain way to please them, make them proud, and to not disappoint them.

Please hear me when I say this: when someone loves you unconditionally, they'll support you in whatever makes you happy, even if that's something they don't personally like or think is manly. And trust me, spending your life trying NOT to disappoint someone will make you miserable. We have to live from a place of love, not fear. Love always wins.

INFLUENCER GROUP 2: FRIENDS

Like your family, your friends typically care about you and want to be there for you. The problem is, they're usually just as focused on trying to be accepted by the guys as you are. Everyone just wants to fit in, no matter how cool or popular they appear to be.

There have been so many times my friends and I accidentally pushed one another into tough situations. No guy wants to be called a girl, or be seen as the wimp or the baby, or be the boy who gets left behind—but they also feel deep down that it's wrong to abandon their friends. Sometimes, the urge to seem cool or popular or like a tough guy wins, and boys ditch their friends and feel bad about it later. Other times, though, they push their friends to "man up" because they don't want to be alone in following these fake rules of manhood. It's way easier to be brave when someone else who is scared is doing it, too, because that way you know you won't be the only one who gets hurt, caught, or in trouble.

Let me let you in on a little secret. Every boy wants to be liked and respected by other boys, especially the boys who say they don't care (I actually think they are the ones who care the most but are the most afraid to show it.). As boys, we are constantly told to stop being emotional and to man up, but the truth is that deep down, underneath all that armor, we all just want to be liked and accepted.

I know for me personally, there were many times growing up when it seemed like the quickest and easiest way to fill ourselves up with confidence was to bring someone else down. But it wasn't, because being cruel and bullying another boy, or pushing a friend to be tougher is kind of like jumping off that bridge. For a moment you may feel powerful, but when you actually reflect on what you've done, you feel terrible. So bullying can seem like a shortcut to making ourselves feel better, stronger, and more manly, but in reality it's a one-way ticket to feeling worse about ourselves than we did in the first place.

While the power we might feel from hurting someone else doesn't last, the effects of our words and actions can sit with the person we've hurt for a very long time—and weigh on our consciences forever. Also I believe bullying and putting others down dims the light in each of us and stunts our spiritual growth. I mean, what could be worse for our souls than making someone else feel bad about themselves and alone? Besides, every religious teacher and prophet in the history of the world has always asked us to treat others the way *we* want to be treated—and doing so builds empathy.

Also, remember when I said that friendship was built on trust? Well, socialization has made it really hard for us boys to trust each other—especially when it comes to our deeper thoughts and feelings. At some point between the ages of six and ten many of our friendships start to feel emotionally unsafe. That's when bullying really starts to rear its ugly head.

> # "BRAVERY IS NOT A QUALITY OF THE BODY, BUT OF THE SOUL."
> ### GANDHI

Have you ever had a friend make fun of you for telling them about something that hurt you or made you afraid? Every time another boy teases us, even if they are joking about something we are going through or feeling, it trains our brains to think those friendships aren't safe, and our bodies will react accordingly. Like your skin might get clammy or your stomach feels sick. Then when we really need to talk to someone about a deep feeling or a problem, our bodies will remember those unsafe feelings we had from before and we'll keep everything that makes us uncomfortable locked inside. Eventually if we don't practice talking and listening to our friends about the things that matter to us, our bodies will instinctively protect our hearts with armor and stop us from feeling not just the bad stuff . . . but EVERYTHING.

Sounds crazy, doesn't it? Well, it's true.

It might sound like I have it all figured out, but the truth is I don't. It took me thirty years—yes, THIRTY years—to realize that I wasn't actually able to talk to my friends about things I was feeling, and even worse, that I had been stopping myself from feeling since I was your age. And guess what? I still struggle with it to this day.

I'll give you an example. You might think one of the hardest things I've ever done in my life was something like climbing a mountain or jumping out of an airplane (which I have done), but actually it was getting the courage to talk to my friends about a deeply personal struggle I was having. A few years ago, I was feeling really down. I actually think I was a bit depressed but didn't know it at the time. I was struggling and knew I needed to talk to my guy friends about it, but every time I picked up the phone to call one of them, I ended up talking myself out of it. I worried they would judge me or think less of me or be too busy to care or that if they knew I was struggling they wouldn't see me as a leader. So instead I devised a plan that would force me to open up. I invited them on a guys' trip to Mexico!

I quickly found out that even thousands of miles away from home, I still couldn't bring myself to talk to them. It was like my body shut down and pretended like everything was fine. All day every day I thought about it, and I kept trying to find the right moment between all the joking and goofing around to talk to my friends about the real reason I planned this trip, but just like before, I would chicken out at the last moment. Just like the day on the bridge, I was afraid to jump, but this time it was my emotional safety that was at risk, and it felt much scarier. The difference was I finally had friends who loved me and who I knew would be there for me without making fun of me, but years of experiencing the opposite and having my weaknesses used against me by boys who said they were my friends had taken its toll. I put up so much armor over my heart that I had forgotten how to trust it.

Then finally, on the last day, it was now or never. Even though I was scared, I knew this was an act of bravery that I

GUT CHECK

PRACTICE OPENING UP

What are some of the things you wish you could tell your friends, but feel like they might not understand? What do you think their reaction might be? On a sheet of paper, write down a list of the harsh things you worry they might say, and on the back write down the list of the supportive things you would hope they say. Be the friend you want to be to yourself first by saying those supportive phrases on your own. Then use them with a friend next time they come to you with a problem.

had to do. This wasn't jumping off a bridge to impress some dudes; it was sharing a part of myself I was scared to show and allowing myself the space to be human.

On that final night, just as I was trying to get myself to jump in and open up, guess what happened? One of my best friends did it first. He broke the ice and brought up something deeply personal that he was struggling with. As I sat there listening to him, I couldn't believe what I was hearing. It felt like he was sharing my story and not his!

As it turns out, my friend had been struggling with the exact thing that was weighing me down (a dependency on porn and a general feeling of hopelessness, which I'll explain more in chapter six). As I heard him share it felt like a massive weight was beginning to lift off my shoulders. I for the first time felt seen and like I wasn't the only one struggling. Soon the other guys responded with love and compassion, which made me feel safe, so I jumped in—heart first!

I opened up and told my friends that I was really scared about this dependency and confused about life. That I felt powerless and hopeless and like a hypocrite. I told them I was feeling super lonely despite all my success and like I was failing at everything. I felt like a bad husband and father and son and brother.

Even though I knew I had so much and so many people who loved me, I couldn't get out of this rut. As soon as I shared it, I felt like a thousand pounds had been lifted off my shoulders. I felt lighter and freer and more like myself than I had in years. Strangely, some of those very feelings disappeared, right there on the spot. Not all of them, but some of them did.

My friends sat there with me and held my pain and worry and fear. And then, one by one, they opened up, too. They started talking about their problems at home, their fears and things they felt guilty or upset about. It was then that I realized that my cool, fun, successful, "manly" friends who I had been comparing myself to for so long were all fighting their own battles and feeling just as insecure as I was. At the end of it all, we agreed that from now on, sharing our feelings and being vulnerable with each other would be a normal thing for us. Because in doing so we felt better—free of pressure, true to ourselves, and most of all, better connected as friends—just by opening up.

Think about that—we're all so afraid about seeming afraid that we don't admit we're afraid . . . to other people who are also afraid! That's what friendship should be, finding other people with whom you can truly open up and be yourself. So remember, if you and your friends can be brave enough to talk about what's really happening in your lives right now and how you really feel, it just might turn out that you're less alone than you think.

Oh and one more thing, if a friend in your life opens up to you, it's important to NOT judge your friend. If you disagree with something they've said or done, before offering your opinion, ask if they want it or if your thoughts would be helpful to them. Sometimes, people just want to be heard, and simply being there for them is the best thing you can do as a friend.

INFLUENCER GROUP 3: PEOPLE WHO BULLY

No one's more obviously scared of their own vulnerability—and how other guys might perceive that weakness—than someone who bullies. There could even be a chance that the person who bullies is YOU. As I said before, I went through periods where I was both being bullied and a bully to other kids to make myself feel more powerful. Remember, some people pick on others because it's the easiest way to show how strong they are, and to distract everyone, but mostly themselves, from their own feelings of inadequacy and worthlessness.

There's a saying I repeat to myself whenever I run into people who bully (especially online), and if you do the same, I think it will help you find compassion and empathy in other tough situations over the course of your life:

Hurt people hurt people.

That means that people who are picking on you or bullying you are doing it because a) they feel bullied by someone in their life, or b) they want to trick themselves into feeling that they're on top, and tougher than others, when in reality they actually feel like they're at the bottom.

The mentality seems to be: *Hey, life sucks sometimes, but at least I'm not that kid I just picked on.*

I want to help people remember that they don't have to put someone else down to build themselves up. But let's be clear: just because someone is hurting doesn't make it okay for them to hurt another person. It's not. This is an explanation, not an excuse. No one should be allowed to lay a hand on you without your permission, and no one should be allowed to make you or the people you care about feel bad or fearful.

I remember being in seventh grade and being terrorized by a boy named Eddie. He would follow me around during lunch and say horrible things to me. Push me, trip me, throw things at me, and spread rumors about me. He was also bigger than me and could physically hurt me. I didn't know what to do or who to talk to. I was so scared of him that I didn't even want to go to school, but I couldn't talk to anyone about it because I didn't want to seem like a wimp—aka a girl.

So I just put up with it, and found myself hiding in between classes or not going out for lunch because I didn't want to get hurt or humiliated. It was terrible. Looking back, I wish I would have gone to a teacher, or told my parents or another adult I felt safe with, that I was scared

HEADS UP! Too many young people are dying by suicide because of bullying. In a recent report, the Center for Disease Control stated that bullying and suicide-related behavior are closely related. That means victims of bullying are more likely to experience high levels of suicide-related behavior than their peers who aren't bullied. It hurts my heart just thinking about it.

None of us know the battles someone is fighting privately, which is why true bravery is standing up for someone instead of staying silent. If you're being bullied, please tell someone right away and make it clear that you're hurting and scared. If you are having thoughts about suicide or harming yourself in any way, please ask for help. You can also call the National Suicide Prevention Lifeline at 800-273-8255. Remember, asking for help is perhaps one of the bravest things you could ever do.

And please, please, PLEASE hear me when I say this: there is nothing that can happen to you that is so bad that it requires ending your life. Nothing. There is always a way out even if at times it feels like your world is ending. I promise you that it can and will get better. We need you here.

instead of pretending I was fine. Then maybe someone at the school or in Eddie's family could have helped him, too. School should be a safe place for everyone, and if it's not we have to say something, even if it means other boys might judge us.

I can't tell you how many times, after either getting tied to a goalpost, tripped on the playground, or called "Boner" in front of a bunch of laughing girls, that I later ended up looking in the mirror and telling myself I was a coward for not standing up to Eddie and fighting back even if it meant getting my butt kicked.

And that's the biggest consequence of bullying—it makes us question our worth and value and turn against ourselves and even worse, if we don't process our pain, it can leak out onto others and we can end up becoming a bully ourselves.

INFLUENCER GROUP 4: THE MEDIA

Man, aren't all those actors on Netflix doing *awesome*? On social media, too. And in magazines. All those supercool people with millions of followers and perfect bodies in those super posed photos, shot with the perfect lighting. There's no way they could be insecure or worried about their skin or body fat percentage. I'm sure none of the people who parade around half-naked on their social profiles are worried about how they look in a bathing suit, or impressing their friends or the people they like. I mean, they must be living their best lives. It must be nice to be so confident and unafraid of the world . . . right? Wrong.

Let's get real. A lot of what you see on social media is artificial and curated. Even the posts by people who are intentionally being real and authentic are planned and calculated most of the time. I try hard to be as sincere as I can on social media, but if you think I'm above redoing a video if I mess up or retaking a picture if I don't like how I look in it, you'd be mistaken. As much as I hate to admit it, just like everyone else, I do care about how the world sees me even when I don't want to.

But why do we all feel that way? Because the media is a massive influencer and one of the strongest sources of fear among young people. Movies, music, sports, and social media often feel tailor-made to make us feel insecure that we're not meeting the standards of manhood and that we're not enough. The media teaches us what it looks like to be a man, and what "bravery" means, and then constantly reinforces that definition.

While the media is tough on men and boys, it's undeniable that girls have gotten it far worse historically. For centuries women have been bombarded with messages to get thinner, thicker, taller, shorter, prettier, *better*. On the other hand, boys have only just started getting their share of negative media input, especially in the age of social media. Today, everyone from a massive pop star to some kid down the block can make you envy their sick abs, awesome car, "perfect" life and even their good deeds at the push of a button—even if they have a normal belly, a bicycle, and a deep-seated fear of what other people think about them. But why show who you really are when you can show who you wish you were?

Listen, it's totally okay to like the things and people that entertain us without questioning them too much, but we also have to acknowledge that people in media do have a stake in keeping us self-conscious and doubting ourselves. This is called a duality, which means two conflicting things can be true at the same time. Companies use streaming and online platforms to sell products through targeted ads that are shown to users based on algorithms that track the content we consume. Social media developers want to make sure we spend as much time as possible on their apps, too, because they make money through selling ad space. Being a successful salesperson means convincing people we need to buy something in order to feel complete, or fill a void in our lives, or even worse, to fear what other people might think of us if we don't have the latest trendy thing. If we honestly

> ## "IF YOU FEEL SOMETHING CALLING YOU TO DANCE OR WRITE OR PAINT OR SING, PLEASE REFUSE TO WORRY ABOUT WHETHER YOU'RE GOOD ENOUGH. JUST DO IT. BE GENEROUS. OFFER A GIFT TO THE WORLD NO ONE ELSE CAN OFFER: YOURSELF."
>
> ### GLENNON DOYLE
>
> BESTSELLING AUTHOR

all felt like we were enough, I think the entire internet and global financial markets would probably collapse!

Take it from me as someone who has been on TV: it's all acting. Even the bodies we see in TV and films aren't realistic. All your favorite superheroes work with expensive personal trainers and do insane diets and work out for hours each day just to get those abs camera ready. Many even resort to using dangerous hormones and drugs like testosterone and HGH (human growth hormone) to give them the extra edge. Some use makeup or CGI (special effects) to have abs drawn on their body if they aren't happy with their results. I know this because I did it! Confession time: for pretty much all my shirtless scenes on *Jane the Virgin*, I'd ask the makeup crew to put a little body makeup on my abs to give them "contour," which is just a fancy way of saying make them look better. But I'll talk more about body image in chapter four.

The point is, even all your favorite influential people have a carefully tailored image (and body) that can be used to encourage you to buy the products they endorse. This is literally the engine that powers social media. The sooner we accept this and understand it, the freer we'll be to use social media as a tool and enjoy it. What I mean is: guardrails can help make us feel safe, and sometimes just simply knowing and understanding WHY something exists is good enough to help keep our behavior and actions in check.

So, if we all understand that one of the purposes of social media is to sell us something, and that many (if not most) people with large followings begin to make money off their followers, we can be more mindful about how we consume content. Think of it like this. When you start a video game, you are *choosing* to play it, but oftentimes we don't think of social media this way. We confuse it with real life, but so often it's not; it's a gamified version of the human experience. This means that every like, comment, and view is documented and recorded by the algorithm to learn what you like and then sell you more of it. Sometimes, we don't realize we are actually the ones being *played*, not the ones playing. I believe that once you know you are in the game and you understand the rules, the more control you have to make decisions for yourself.

And look, there is nothing wrong with making money or selling something to an audience—even I do it with my followers. It's one of the ways I support my family, and this book is one of the things I will be using my social media to help sell. At the same time, I believe those of us with platforms have a responsibility to promote things that are healthy/good/in line with our values because there is so much power that comes with influence, and as Uncle Ben said to Spider-Man, "With great power comes great responsibility."

Here's another thing that's good to remember: the "manly" men you see smiling for the cameras are more than likely also insecure about some part of the way they look or feel, and maybe are even worried about staying relevant. They are; we all are . . . because we're human and not designed to be walking, talking billboards. We are so much more than that, and since we live in a world that oftentimes values profits over people, the brave thing to do is block out the media noise and form our own opinions of who we are or how we should be.

YOU'VE BEEN THE BRIDGE ALL ALONG

When we talk about men being "brave" or "courageous," we usually have a lot of preconceived ideas in mind. Like we talked about earlier, bravery is generally associated with taking some sort of physical risk. But oftentimes, even those physical acts of bravery aren't really brave—they're responses to fear. Fear of not being seen as brave. Pretty confusing, right? That an act of bravery can actually be motivated by

INFLUENCE IS KING

Grab a notebook and draw something in your life that you like because you saw someone else—a friend or an athlete or someone in a movie—like it first, such as a phrase you say a lot, or a piece of clothing you wear, or a food you eat. If tomorrow it wasn't cool anymore, would you still like it? Write down why or why not.

fearing we won't be seen as brave. Who would have thought the cool kid who jumped first from the bridge was actually super scared? Maybe not of the jump, but of not being seen as cool or brave.

So he took the physical risk to be liked and admired, to be seen as enough. Sure, some people love to do wild and risky things, but many times it's that fear that makes us jump. That's not the sort of bravery I want us to make room for in our hearts. In fact, that's the kind of bravery I wish I could unlearn. There's a different sort of bravery, though—the bravery to acknowledge and accept how you *really* feel. That kind of bravery could help us enjoy life a little more if we're willing to practice it.

The bravery to tell your friends when you're hurting inside.

The bravery to apologize right away when you've done something that hurt someone or that you regret.

The bravery to tell other boys to stop being cruel, or creepy, or mean.

The bravery to ask an influential man in your life what he really means when he says boys "need to be *tough*," or to "quit being a girl" and "man up."

So be brave, my friend. Be brave for the boy looking in the mirror who realizes that he doesn't like or believe in the things those other boys say. The kid who knows that it's okay to feel what he feels. Who knows that being called a girl isn't something to be afraid of or insulted by.

Be brave for the kid on the bridge who doesn't want to jump. Don't make him.

BREAKING IT DOWN

THE RULES OF BEING BRAVE AREN'T REAL.

There are going to be moments when people try to convince you that you're not manly, or tough, or brave unless you do something to prove it. But being pressured into doing something is the least brave thing of all.

OTHERS AROUND YOU WILL INFLUENCE YOU TO BELIEVE THEM.

We're being influenced on all sides by people and forces telling us to act and behave a certain way. It's our job to see them for what they are and make decisions from a grounded place of self-awareness and love. Not from fear.

THERE'S NO SHAME IN SAYING NO.

At the end of the day, if something scares or upsets you, you don't have to do it. Being true to yourself and setting your own standards makes you a stronger person than just doing what everyone else is doing.

IT'S BRAVE TO ASK FOR HELP.

Sometimes the bravest thing you can do is put your ego aside and ask someone you trust for help.

BEING BRAVE IS HARD WORK.

Being brave enough to stand up for yourself and others can be tough, and it's going to take some time to get it down. But if you stay true to what you feel and believe, you'll benefit more than you would otherwise and eventually make the true meaning of brave super cool.

BE BRAVE—WHEN YOU'RE READY.

Overcoming your fears is important—but it has to be on your own terms and when you are ready. Anyone who forces you to do something you aren't ready to do isn't trying to help you . . . they are trying to help themselves.

2

BOYS WILL BE
SMART

JUSTIN VS. SHIRTLESS GUY

Not too long ago, there was a period of my life where there was no Justin—I was simply "The Shirtless Guy on TV."

For the better part of the last eighteen years, I've been shirtless on TV. From my first big role on the medical TV show *Everwood* until I played Rafael on the romantic comedy series *Jane the Virgin*, I have had to take my shirt off constantly. The body image issues I'd suffered growing up—don't worry, we'll get there in chapter four—had caused me to hit the weight room, hard, and suddenly my entire sense of self was built around my body, both in my personal life and in my work life as an actor. After a while, it just kind of became my identity, and I let it.

Eventually I realized that I was being used more like a prop or a way to set up jokes. Like during one scene in *Everwood*, two characters were talking and they had my character studying while doing push-ups in the background. And while I must say it was pretty funny, it became more and more clear that my value to Hollywood back then was overwhelmingly tied to my physical appearance, not my talent.

As an up-and-coming actor, this affected me in ways I didn't even realize until later on. I felt like I'd only gotten the role because of how I looked, not because I was a good actor. The joke of me being ripped and muscular and always having my shirt off was getting old. I would soon start feeling insecure that no one would ever take me seriously as anything more than eye candy. I had a brain and a heart, too! But I felt like no one could see it. (And yes, I know how cringeworthy that can sound coming from someone like me, but this whole book is about truth, and that's my truth.)

For years I tried to prove to Hollywood that I was more than just "The Shirtless Guy." That experience gave me insight, empathy, and compassion for what women experience every day. Girls and women are treated very different than boys and men in the world (especially in the entertainment business).

How? Well, for example, as a man, no one ever bossed me around or threatened my job if I gained weight or my hair started graying. Unfortunately, that happens to actresses all the time. And while the press sometimes wrote things about me that I didn't like—a GQ article once said men (who play fathers) with bodies like mine on TV could lead real-world fathers "down a path towards extreme dieting, exercise addiction, and generally toxic habits"—they never made me out to be stupid just because I was in good shape. The fact that I was "Shirtless Guy" may have made me feel insecure about my intelligence, but my intelligence was never called into question or talked about often.

Women, on the other hand, get their intelligence questioned *constantly*. If they're conventionally beautiful, the thought is that they probably get by on their looks, and because most women on average make less money than men for doing the exact same job with the exact same level of education (this is called the gender pay gap), many women have to work twice as hard to be taken seriously.

Men, meanwhile, well, we don't have to really *do* anything to be taken seriously. According to the script of masculinity, men *are* smart (even if we're not). We somehow know the answers (even when we don't), and we are just naturally confident (even when we aren't).

This, to be real, sucks. It's a lose-lose equation. Girls either have to work twice as hard to get the same respect as boys or have to dumb themselves down to please others who are intimidated by them. Meanwhile, men are always expected to know the right answer or act as if they do. And we often get a free pass when we don't.

By the way, it's okay for women to be smarter than men! And it's more than okay to have female role models in your life. I admire so many women who are smarter than me. My wife, Emily; one of my best friends in the world, Noelle; my amazing cohost on the *Man Enough* podcast, Liz Plank; the list could go on and on. In fact, there is no way this book would exist without the smart women who give me feedback and push me to both *be* better and *do* better. I never feel insecure or like I am less of a man, because I help them be better and do better, too. It's never a one-way street.

All right, let me ask you this: Think about your life right now. Do you know everything you're supposed to? Are you sure of everything?

Me either. And if I'm unsure about the world around me today, you can bet that as a boy, I also had no idea about everything I am telling you now. Even after all these years I feel like I am JUST starting to get it.

But THAT is a good thing. The less we know, the more chances we have to learn. The more we learn, the more we understand about the world, ourselves, and how to operate in it. I actually think not knowing the right answer is awesome. Who says we have to always know the answer anyway? There is so much to learn in the world, and the only way we can learn is by being curious. and admitting what we don't know. Isn't it interesting that some of the smartest people who have ever lived have said that in the grand scheme of the universe, they felt like they knew nothing? In fact, it is rumored that Albert Einstein once said that *the only thing you absolutely have to know is the location of the library*.

That's why the idea of boys and men feeling like we need to be smart from the get-go, or even worse, that we don't need to be smart at all because we are men, is a problem. If boys are supposed to already know something and we *don't*, we worry that we're stupid. We get self-conscious. We try to act like we're smart to keep the other men from thinking we aren't, or we play it cool and dumb ourselves down and make fun of the kid who is smarter than us. We make decisions without the right information, and later, while we're regretting our bad decisions, we wonder why we didn't just admit that we didn't know something in the first place!

TO KNOW OR NOT TO KNOW

Ask yourself: Can someone who thinks they have nothing left to learn *really* be that smart? Can someone be intelligent if they stop themselves from learning new things? Do you feel smarter when you don't know something and make up an answer, or do you feel smarter when you say you don't know the answer but are willing to then learn about it?

If that weren't confusing enough . . . there isn't just one type of smart. But don't worry, we're going to talk about that. You've got this. Or maybe you don't. Confused? Even better.

THE DIFFERENT TYPES OF SMARTS, AKA INTELLIGENCES

On paper, being intelligent or "smart" might just mean knowing textbook information or being well-read. Often this kind of intelligence is casually known as being "book smart"—the information you learn at school, like history, math, science, literature. Book smarts are important because they allow you to better understand the world and can help with getting a job in a specific field. But what's important to remember is that there are other types of intelligence that matter just as much. Just because you may not be the best reader, or have the longest attention span, doesn't mean you aren't smart!

Another example of an intelligence that has more to do with situational and environmental awareness is what many people call "street smarts." Street smarts are about knowing the basics of connecting with everyday people in a way that allows you to get by or survive—how to talk to certain people, how to get the best food in certain neighborhoods, how to tell if someone's lying, who you can or can't trust when you need a ride home, etc. Street smarts involve a mixture of instinct, experience, and a general knowledge of humanity.

Another kind of intelligence is called "emotional intelligence" or "heart smarts" (although I've never heard anyone say "heart smarts"). It's also known by what businesses call "EQ." If IQ (intelligence quotient) is all about book smarts, then EQ is about emotional smarts. Someone with good EQ can understand a person's motivations, wants, and needs just by talking to them and, more important, by listening. They often have high levels of empathy and compassion. In fact, a recent study by the website PsychTests even showed that people with high EQ levels did better at their jobs, got into fewer arguments, and were more satisfied with their daily lives.

To this day, the public school system is traditionally focused on helping its students develop book smarts. It's actually one of the reasons school was so hard for me growing up. I often felt like I wasn't smart enough because the way I learned was so different than the way school required me to learn. The good news is that this is changing quickly—more and more public schools are embracing alternate teaching methods and recognizing diverse talents and learning abilities in their students.

When I was a kid, no one ever called me "book smart." I was antsy and literally couldn't sit still at a desk (I still can't. . . . That's why I'm standing as I write this). I got average grades in high school, was never a very good test taker, and attended college on a partial athletic scholarship. And while I know now that book smarts are only one part of the equation, I never received that message in school. I was given the impression that book smarts were all that mattered. The result? I consistently felt unintelligent, dumb, or less than my classmates when it came to my ability as a student, which translated into feeling like I wasn't enough outside the classroom as well. Where do those feelings lead for me and many other men?

You guessed it: overcompensation. "Overcompensating" is when you overdo trying to prove something because you're actually lacking in other parts of your life. The easiest example of this is material possessions: someone who feels like they aren't big or smart or cool or handsome enough buys a super expensive car, or a flashy watch, or the most expensive pair of shoes they can find. Instead of dealing with their own problems or feelings, they try to quick-fix them or hide them by going way too far. I overcompensated everywhere—cracking jokes, working out, trying to be cool—all because I felt unintelligent.

> ## "A GOOD HEAD AND GOOD HEART ARE ALWAYS A FORMIDABLE COMBINATION."
>
> **NELSON MANDELA**

Over the course of my education, I had to constantly look for ways to keep up with the class. Deep down I wanted so badly to excel at school and to be seen as a smart kid because I knew that the things I really wanted to do in my life required intelligence. But the truth was that the way my brain best learned information didn't always fit with how information was being taught.

For example, I was an athlete, and sports were a huge part of my life growing up. I basically lived for soccer and I was the happiest when I was outside and moving my body. When I was in class sitting at my desk, I would often count down the minutes until recess, and I remember making any excuse I could to leave my desk and use the bathroom even if I didn't have to. I'm sure everyone thought I had a bladder problem, but that was a small price to pay for a few moments of freedom!

See, no one had ever taught me how to be still, or use my breath to calm my mind, or ways to absorb information by taking notes. So sitting in class without movement for me felt like torture. While I know a lot of kids don't feel this way or have these issues, there are many who also do. I always had a hard time absorbing information by just listening and would get easily distracted and start daydreaming if I didn't find the subject my teacher was talking about interesting.

Tim is struggling with the way a teacher is teaching but is too afraid to admit it. He feels like everyone else in his class understands but him. What do you think Tim should do? Ask his teacher for help after class? Keep his problems to himself and try to work it out on his own? Write your answer down and include what you'd say to Tim if he was your friend.

I also had a wild imagination, which as I got older has made me successful in my career, but when I was younger and in school, it only got me in trouble. And I got in trouble a lot. I think half the time it was just because I needed some excitement or stimulation. The other half was just because I needed attention and wanted to be noticed. One time in fourth grade I told my teacher my dad was a lawyer and he'd sue her if she didn't let me go to the bathroom. That didn't work out too well for me.

Learning is an ongoing process, and even if being book

smart isn't your strongest type of intelligence, a certain level of knowledge in math, history, science, and literature is really helpful in life. But what's even more helpful is figuring out how you can make the process of learning easier. You might never need to use geometry or algebra in your life again, but adapting to situations that are challenging and deepening your level of understanding about how you learn and absorb information is something you will use forever. And don't forget, there are great teachers out there who understand different ways of learning and will work hard to help you no matter how you learn.

But just because you have a hard time memorizing dates or complex math equations doesn't mean you're stupid. Just because you struggle taking written tests doesn't mean you're not smart. It's okay to not know and to need help. It's okay to raise your hand and say, "I'm not sure I get this. Is there another way to explain it?" It's also okay to feel embarrassed about not getting it. But don't hold that in . . . share it with your teacher after class or before school one day. Hopefully they will be smart enough themselves to find a way to make you feel better and help you learn. (Remember, there are tons of super successful people who didn't do well in school. You are not alone. Your test scores will not dictate your future. Trust me.)

Actually, now that I think about it, you know what's kind of funny? All the things that got me in trouble as a child, and what led to countless embarrassing parent-teacher conferences with my mom and dad, have ultimately become some of the very things that have helped me succeed in my life. I have to believe that a good part of both my personal and professional growth has come from the ability to multitask. To do multiple things at once and to also know when to give my undivided attention to something and focus on a single task.

Of course, at times my restlessness has really frustrated me. I have had moments where I wished I could be more like the people who can sit and read a book for eight hours at a time, but I also have to appreciate and understand my mind and body, the way I was created. And what's even cooler is that now that I'm in my thirties, I'm learning tips and tricks I never knew before that help me focus, and I've found that all this time I really wasn't different, I just didn't know what my body needed to be able to sit, be still, and focus on one task at a time. Things like breathwork, meditation, and mindfulness have been so helpful for me.

MEDITATION 101

Meditation might look different to each of us, but I think of it as the act of quieting your mind and letting the noise of everyday life drift away so you can be more aware of your thoughts and feelings. It really helps you find a sense of calm and focus. Meditation can take many forms, like taking slow deep breaths, saying affirmations, moving or connecting with your body, or simply closing your eyes and imagining you're someplace quiet and serene. I try to meditate and pray every day. It's an essential part of my mental health tool kit. Meditating doesn't mean you have to be still either. Sometimes I take short walks where I focus on my breath, and other times I take cold showers, which forces my racing mind to only focus on one thing: breathing. For me, I've learned the combination of slow movement and breathing works the best—and when I really need it, that boost of cold-water clarity—but everyone, and every mind, is different. Also, if you are interested in meditation or learning about breathwork, there are tons of awesome apps you can download on your (or your parent's phone) to get you started. (Now, if only they had taught me all that in school, I might have had all As. And even if I didn't, I would have been happier for sure!)

ASKING DIRECTIONS: WHAT WILL THE OTHER GUYS THINK?!

I know you probably can't drive yet, but can you imagine a time when people drove and didn't use their iPhone, GPS, and things like Google Maps to get to their destination? Back then, for men driving anywhere was either a hassle or an adventure. Either you had that family member who could perfectly read a road map and tell you where to go, or you ended up two towns away from your destination, wondering where you made the wrong turn.

But there was a third option, of course: asking someone for directions. Yeah. Not for my dad, though. While my dad is so much better at it now, it was clear that asking for directions was like admitting defeat in a wrestling match. Sometimes it seemed like it would have been better to drive our family directly into the ocean or through a dangerous mountain range in the middle of a blizzard that almost left us stuck for days because he thought it was a shortcut (true story).

My dad wasn't alone, either. A study by TrekAce, a company that makes GPS navigational aids, found that the average British man will travel nine hundred additional, unnecessary miles over the course of fifty years. And even after realizing they are lost, only 6 percent of the men polled would check a map or ask for help. C'mon, fellas; that means that for every hundred men who get lost, only six of us are willing to ask for directions.

The thing is, this idea wasn't strange for me. Even when I was young, asking for directions was something that I just never saw men do. And it's not really about asking for directions anymore, because now that we all have smartphones we rarely ever got lost. There's a deeper issue here . . . an issue that affects every area of our lives. Most boys are taught— whether we realize it or not—that asking for help makes us look weak. It's like there's an unwritten (and ridiculous) rule of masculinity that says that you have to know everything, right down to which way is north, and if somebody assists you, then you really didn't get there on your own, which somehow makes you less of a man.

My grandpa Loui, who passed away before I was born, was an Italian immigrant who became a senator in Indiana despite facing prejudice and discrimination. A few years ago, I learned from my aunt that not long after my grandfather had lost reelection in the senate, he had fallen on hard financial times. The car factory he had worked at since he was young had abruptly shut down and he not only lost his job, but also his retirement fund. He was left with nothing. At one point he ended up working nights as a janitor to make ends meet and keep the lights on for his family.

While my grandfather struggled during that time, despite having helped countless people in his town, he himself was too proud to ask for help. I can only imagine the heaviness of his heart and the loneliness he must have felt as he suffered in silence with no one to talk to or turn to. My aunt even felt embarrassed telling me about it over sixty years later. The messages of masculinity tell us to quietly suffer, never reach out for help or show vulnerability. The fear of what other people might think can throw us completely off course, too. When we're unsure of ourselves, we might quietly suffer sometimes, and other times we might act like we don't need help at all, that we have everything under control, and that we know everything, even if we're wrong.

This failure to admit we're wrong or don't know something can also turn into mansplaining. Essentially, "mansplaining" is when a guy lectures or educates a woman on something she already knows about. For example, in high school, one of my teammates insisted to two female classmates that girls and women had menopause every month and go through their period later in life (the girls were *not* impressed). Now, while I don't know exactly what was going through the guy's head,

78

I can imagine that it had nothing to do with impressing the girls (which he clearly was not doing) and more to do with looking like an expert in front of the rest of us.

To this day I still have conversations with some of my best friends where we talk in absolute circles trying to prove that we're right, when in reality we are just making stuff up or arguing for the sake of arguing. Now, that can be harmless fun when it's between close friends, but we have to be mindful to not turn that same energy into harm and carry that harm into the world.

For a long time, I felt like I had to be right to have value in the world. I was so afraid of being seen as less than that I would try to make sure I was right in every situation I was in, even when I was so clearly wrong. I would feel embarrassed or like a fool if I was ever corrected, and I did whatever I could to feel powerful because deep down Real Me felt powerless.

Convincing someone else they are wrong for the sake of your own ego (even if they are right) is especially tough on women and girls. This behavior is called "gaslighting," which basically means trying to make someone believe that their experience of reality isn't real and true to the point where they doubt their sanity. An example could be a person saying something like "It's a sunny day today" when there are

> # "ALL STREAMS FLOW TO THE OCEAN BECAUSE IT IS LOWER THAN THEY ARE. HUMILITY GIVES THE OCEAN ITS POWER."
>
> ### ◀ LAO TZU ▶
> #### AUTHOR OF THE *TAO TE CHING*

no clouds in the sky, and their friend responding, "No, it's not. What's wrong with you? It's obviously cloudy. How can you not see that?"

Gaslighting can happen to boys, too. I experienced it in my first real relationship (which I'll talk about more in chapter six). I was made to feel like I was just imagining things all the time and couldn't think straight. Even when I found out she was cheating on me, I was convinced that I was a terrible boyfriend. It was awful.

If you're ever in a similar situation, I suggest walking away and talking to an adult about it. They might not have all the answers—none of us do—but they can always listen and remind you that if someone else needs to make you doubt yourself so they can feel superior, being with them is not worth harming your mental health.

THE RIGHT SIDE OF WRONG

One quality that I don't feel is talked about enough as it relates to masculinity is the importance of humility. There's something so empowering about being humble and admitting you don't know the answer, or that the answer you currently have is wrong. Sure, there might be an initial moment where it's uncomfortable—I think we can agree that being right feels good, and being wrong, or misinformed, doesn't—but once that wave of self-criticism passes, the hunger of curiosity can take its place. By humbling yourself and sitting in the discomfort of not knowing, I believe something almost spiritual happens, and regardless of who you are, you become real and relatable. Every person on this planet can identify with the universal truths and feelings of being confused, making mistakes, and being wrong, even the ones who appear to be always right. Growing up as a boy, I felt like everyone seemed to value traits like power, force, certainty, and decisiveness more than humility. Now I know that humility is something we should all be embracing because it gives us a greater capacity to learn and grow as a human. I like to think of humility as a glass filled with rocks. At first, it may seem like the glass is full and there is no room for anything else to be put in it because the rocks go all the way to the top. But the glass actually *isn't* full because there is room in between the rocks!

Now imagine *we* are the glass and *everything we know* is the rocks. Sometimes we think we have a full cup, but if we are humble and admit that we don't know everything, we can make room for even more knowledge, empathy, power, and so much more to fill our hearts and minds. (Also, when you pour small pebbles into a jar full of rocks it doesn't overflow, because the pebbles fill the spaces between the rocks. And what's even cooler is that while it might not look like it, there is even more room between the pebbles! Sand can be poured in and fill even the small spaces! Mind blown, right?)

There's a moment from high school that I'll never forget. It was my senior year, and I needed a passing grade, so I was forced to do the unthinkable: ask a teacher for help. We were assigned to complete a book report that would make up a huge percentage of our final grade. I liked reading, but I had trouble retaining the information I read, something I struggle with to this day when I don't prepare my mind and my body to be still. I'd sit down, crack the book, read a few sentences, and then think about making movies in my head, or about the pizza I had for lunch, or the big soccer game that week.

Boom, ten minutes go by and I'd realize I had just read ten pages but had no idea what had happened. Then there was also the issue of getting my thoughts from my head to the paper, and to do that meant I had to sit down, be still, and type, which honestly felt like having to run a marathon (something I have felt quite a few times writing this book).

When I asked my teacher, Ms. Reed, for help, she took a completely different approach than most of my other teachers had. She talked with me, listened to me, and challenged me to complete the assignment in a way that excited me. She was actually the first teacher to teach me about the different types of intelligences I talked about earlier in this chapter. We brainstormed together and decided that the best way for me to complete the assignment was a video book report. I didn't have to type; I didn't have to get my thoughts from my head to the paper; and, best of all, I got to tap into my love of creating, acting, and making really cheesy movies with my dad's camera.

I got an A on the assignment, but more important, I got the first taste of my own capabilities. I realized I wasn't dumb, and I had never *been* dumb. I just learned differently. But the first step to learning that was admitting that I needed help and asking for it. If I'd never been smart enough to admit that I didn't know the answer, I would've walked away knowing even less.

> # "I WAS BORN TO MAKE MISTAKES, NOT FAKE PERFECTION."
>
>  **DRAKE**
>
> **RAPPER, SINGER, AND ACTOR**

Asking for help, input, or advice is a muscle. Early on, I was given a lot of opportunities to exercise that muscle. But the only way I could begin to grow that muscle was to take the first step and admit that I didn't know what to do.

My ego had bolstered my armor for so long because egos like armor—a safe, self-contained environment where no one questions them. But the more I put my ego on the line and admitted I didn't know what to do, the better I got at school, at dealing with problems at home, my job, and, most important, in my relationships.

That inner critic of mine was also a lot quieter. I didn't beat myself up as much or compare myself to other people. I felt strong in a way I never did before because it takes true strength to admit when you don't know.

YOU'LL NEVER KNOW—SO YOU HAVE TO KEEP ASKING

One of my favorite comics will always be X-Men, because it's about a group of people with different abilities coming together to fight as one. Every member of the team has their own special power, and it's usually only when they stop thinking they're the best and ask their teammate for help that they can defeat any villain or find a solution to any problem. And sometimes, it's the power they least expect that helps them overcome—suddenly, Wolverine's claws or Storm's weather powers are useless, and only Jubilee's firecracker fingers will do. To me, the X-Men can teach us a valuable lesson: if we could only realize that we are already superheroes in our own right, we would see that our true power lies in our ability to ask each other for help.

But on top of that, the X-Men have one common enemy: ignorance. The world around them fears them for being different, whether that's due to the extent of their powers (Professor X being able to enter anyone's mind) or their physical appearance (Nightcrawler looking like a blue devil). So even as the X-Men defeat evil mutants, robots, and monsters, they are constantly adapting to a world in which some people still refuse to understand them.

Similarly, learning is an ongoing process. No matter how educated, thoughtful, or well-liked we are, there's always room to learn more. Being humble in our knowledge is the only way we can become better as people. And as new ideas are accepted more and more in our society, there will be new things to learn. People will tell us their stories that we've never heard before, because they finally feel safe in describing *their* experiences. The most hurtful thing we can do is say, "You're wrong" or "I've never heard of that. That's not what I was taught!" Instead, we can have the thoughtfulness to say, "Wow, I've never heard of that. I'd love to learn more."

That doesn't mean it's easy, especially for boys, who

> ## "OBSTACLES **DON'T** HAVE TO **STOP** YOU. IF YOU RUN INTO A WALL, **DON'T** TURN AROUND AND GIVE UP. FIGURE OUT HOW TO **CLIMB** IT, GO **THROUGH** IT, OR WORK AROUND IT."
>
> **MICHAEL JORDAN**

have been taught their whole lives that they need to just automatically know everything. It's still something I struggle with to this day. I notice that if I'm not mindful, my first reaction to a friend or anyone telling me that something I said was misinformed, ignorant, or just wasn't *right* is to be defensive and puff up my chest.

Luckily, I have learned to take a breath and let that reaction pass, but sometimes that insecurity still wins. Even when confronted with something I don't understand, I can

THE CONFIDENCE TEST

Having confidence feels amazing, but if it doesn't truly come from within, then it's likely to disappear the moment it's challenged. Think about a moment recently where you lost your confidence. Remember what happened to make your confidence drop and write down why. Was it because you felt embarrassed? Were you comparing yourself to someone else? Were you feeling insecure? The big takeaway from this exercise is to drive home the message that real confidence comes from a deep knowing that you as a person are enough just as you are and that will never fade.

still feel the insecure boy inside me put his walls up and feel like I'm not enough just because I don't know. But I am learning to reframe those moments as invitations and ask questions and become smarter for it. Sure, I can defeat little villains along the way—things I've said, messages society has taught me—but the big bad enemy, ignorance, is still always there. Lurking in the shadows and waiting for the moment where my ego obstructs my sight to take control.

With that in mind, let's stop comparing intellects all the time. Worrying about someone else being less intelligent, or more intelligent, or wiser, or quicker, is a waste of time that could be better spent learning. Who cares if we don't know the right answer and that other people do? If he or she or they are willing to help teach you, great. If not, you are more than capable of teaching yourself.

One last thing before we move on: the goal of being "the best" at something doesn't really help any of us. In reality it's impossible to become the best at something, and even if we did become one of the .00000009 percent of people who really are the best it will only be for a brief moment because soon someone else will dethrone us and become the best. Author and professor Adam Grant really nails it with this powerful observation: "Striving to be the best is a mistake. It creates an illusion of an endpoint—and a delusion that you can only succeed by beating others. Striving to be better shifts the focus from victory to mastery. You're competing with your past self and raising the bar for your future self."

It may seem like a simple change in mindset, but it's actually really profound. Once we realize the idea of being the best at everything is unrealistic and gets in the way of our happiness, we can let it go and start learning how to be the best versions of ourselves.

BREAKING IT DOWN

THE EXPECTATION THAT BOYS SHOULD KNOW EVERYTHING IS UNFAIR.

Boys are socialized to believe they should never admit they're wrong, or that they don't know something. But how are boys supposed to learn *anything* if they have to pretend that they know *everything*?

YOU CAN BE SMART IN DIFFERENT WAYS.

There isn't one type of smart—there are book smarts, street smarts, and heart smarts. Just because you haven't mastered one doesn't mean you're unintelligent—you just learn differently.

REFUSING TO ADMIT WE'RE WRONG LEAVES US LOST.

Like guys not wanting to ask for directions, acting like we know where we're going only sends us driving around aimlessly. But the sooner we can ask for help, the sooner we can get back on track.

LET'S ALL ADMIT WE DON'T KNOW EVERYTHING.

Once we start admitting that we don't know everything, we can stop comparing our intellects and each learn in the ways that work best for our unique self. And the best part? We can feel less alone in the process!

3

BOYS WILL BE
COOL

MY WALK OF PAIN

Sixth and seventh grades were really confusing and painful for me. Not so much physically, but emotionally. In sixth grade I was four foot eleven and a few inches shorter than a lot of the other guys and a half foot shorter than many of the girls. A few of the other boys had hit puberty before me, and I started getting teased just because my body wasn't there yet.

All I wanted was to fit in, and during this super awkward period, hitting puberty "late" (as it turns out, I was right on time) was pretty much the worst thing ever. So to fit in I got creative and started experimenting with ridiculous methods to fake puberty, which, looking back, are so embarrassing I can't believe I'm writing about them! But hey, at least I'm man enough to be honest about my insecurities, right?

When I started seventh grade, I remember changing my voice (on purpose) to squeak every now and then just so I'd sound like the other guys' slightly deeper, raspy, pubescent voices. It worked, too. Every time someone would laugh at me or tell me my voice was changing, it would make me feel good because I sounded just like the other guys. But just underneath that good feeling was a stronger feeling of sadness. Sadness that I had to change my voice in the first place, sadness that I didn't like who I was, anger toward my body for being "slower" than my friends', and shame that I wasn't enough, just because a few of the other guys hit puberty before me.

And it gets worse. Later that year I remember going into the bathroom at lunch with a couple of guys. They were looking in the mirror and popping their zits and laughing about how far the white pus went. So gross. I was watching them from the sink a few feet away when they turned around and said, "Ah, don't worry, Baldoni, maybe one day you'll hit puberty," and then walked out of the bathroom, laughing.

That moment in the bathroom, seeing those boys laughing about a shared experience, as disgusting and immature as it was, made me feel like there was something wrong with me. I wanted to be like them instead of feeling left out and left behind. So I went home and started doing things to clog my pores and give myself zits. I took some of my mom's super thick oily night cream that she used to prevent wrinkles and started putting it all over my face at night.

Guess what? It worked. Too well, actually. I got acne so bad that years later in high school I ended up having to go on the most intense acne medication ever. But hey, I fit in, so the performance was worth it . . . right?

Another thing that I was super insecure about was my walk. One day I was walking to class from recess after a game of touch football (or more like "shove the guy as hard as you can" football) and noticed two of the popular guys who I wanted to be close friends looking back at me, chuckling and whispering to each other. Hoping they weren't laughing at me, I caught up to them and asked them what they were laughing at. They looked at each other and then said, "You! Why are you walking like that? You walk weird. Stop trying to walk like us . . . just walk normal, dude."

To this day, I hate watching myself walk. I feel like I have a waddle. In truth it's known as a soccer player's walk, which is a gait that a lot of us soccer players have because of our tight hips (if you watch a professional soccer game now, you won't be able to not see it). But I hate it. It feels like there's something wrong with me. It feels like I don't walk like a man because in seventh grade the other boys told me I didn't. What's even worse is that my dad has the same walk as I do, and when I was growing up, I was mad at him for giving me this walk. How could he do this to me?

Maybe those guys actually gave me some good advice. Maybe I *was* trying too hard to be like them. At the time, though, all I heard was just that I'd *never* be like them, I'd just be like *me*. And that meant being uncool. Not enough. And that *crushed* me.

"Cool." It's such a vague word, but as a boy, I had this bone-deep understanding of what it meant. "Cool" meant

> ## "HAPPINESS IS LIKE BEING COOL. THE HARDER YOU TRY, THE LESS IT'S GOING TO HAPPEN."
>
> ### MARK MANSON
> #### AUTHOR

people knew you and talked about you. "Cool" meant that you always had a table to sit at during lunch, or friends to hang out with on the weekends. "Cool" meant people wanted to spend time with you, came to your birthday party, or told stories about you that might not be true (it was even better if they weren't—you know you're cool if people are so invested in you that they make stuff up about you). In a lot of ways, "cool" and "popular" were the same—cool kids were popular, and being popular in middle school and high school, man, that was cool as hell.

But at the end of the day, "cool" only meant one thing: confidence. Being cool meant knowing you were cool, or at least never doubting that you were cool. All the things we traditionally assign to cool guys—new clothes, the newest iPhone, a great taste in music, the attention of every person in your grade—were all things that inspired confidence in a guy.

In my younger brain, that's what the guys whose walk I was imitating had. Of course, what I didn't know was that confidence, *true* confidence, doesn't just happen when everything's going great . . . and if it does, that confidence can be super fleeting the first time something goes wrong. Real confidence comes from the inside, and a deep knowing that no matter what anyone thinks, you belong and you are enough. It takes a lot of hard soul-searching, personal honesty, conflicted emotions, and, if we're being real, often lots of crying, to become confident with who you really are. But like intelligence, strength, and so many other things that take hard work, men are told to just *have* it. It's assumed that as a boy, you should automatically be confident. No one stops to ask what's wrong or tries to help you work through your issues—instead, it's "Suck it up, stand up straight, and be cool. Be a man."

In high school, I figured it was all the superficial stuff—clothes, jokes, the walk, the talk—that made you cool. So I worked on my image instead of myself. Spoiler: I did not become cool. Far from it. At least not then.

JUSTIN TRIES TO BE COOL: A TRAGEDY IN THREE PARTS

My walk was just the beginning for me. If I was going to "make it" in high school—as though being a student was a career skill I wanted to master—my first step was to be like the popular kids. I'd pick up mannerisms, phrases, opinions, tips, and tricks from the guys I perceived as confident. I worked my butt off trying to hit that sweet spot, that

THE COOL TEST

This exercise is done well in a group. But it requires trust. Now everyone has to close their eyes. No exceptions. With eyes closed, ask everyone to raise their hand if they have ever felt like they don't fit in. Now open your eyes. If everyone is being honest you will notice that because no one is judging them . . . pretty much every hand is up. Interesting, right? What does it mean to fit in if no one actually feels like they do? How many of the kids that you think of as cool don't even see themselves as cool? For bigger groups, doing this as a secret ballot also works— everyone put a scrap of paper with their oddest quality or biggest insecurity in a hat. The more of these anonymous notes you read, the more you'll understand that everyone worries about the same things you do. Everyone feels like they don't fit in.

perfect place where I was cool (imagine if I'd applied myself half this much to my homework or even to soccer).

And then, one day, it happened. My worst nightmare. A girl I liked told me, "Justin, everyone thinks you're cocky. And honestly, you're kind of full of yourself."

Boom. Direct hit. Destroyed inside!

Full of yourself—like confidence, only bad. Confident for the wrong reasons. Confident, but maybe not deservedly so.

But here's where she missed the mark. I was exactly the opposite of *full of myself*—I was empty of myself and full of everyone else! When it was brought to my attention that I came off as overly confident, it felt totally bizarre, because all I felt were my deep-seated insecurities. So much of my personality (if I can even call it mine) was a big performance. What I learned recently through years of therapy and healing is that over the course of my life I had essentially crowdsourced my own personality. It was like I was creating a piece of music, but all the notes and lyrics were taken from other songs. None of them were mine. The end result might be beautiful, but it didn't feel like I'd made it. It felt foreign, inauthentic . . . fake.

Back then, other people might have seen an arrogant teenager who would interject himself into conversations and make stupid jokes about everything. What they wouldn't have seen, what I managed to keep hidden, is that the same kid would go home at night, exhausted from pretending all day—pretending not to be hurt by the jabs his friends made about him, pretending not to feel sad that the girl he liked thought he was cocky, pretending that finding food in his braces at the end of every day wasn't embarrassing. Pretending to like the zits that formed all over his face and his walk that screamed he was trying too hard. Pretending to be confident when he had no idea how confidence even felt.

Luckily, I have an awesome mom. She understood from her own experiences what it was like to be picked on, and she always gave me the space to cry—to feel whatever I was feeling. I'm so grateful for her and her ability to listen while also constantly reminding me that I was good enough, smart enough, and a person who had more value than what other kids thought of me.

But I felt like I could only go to my mom so much. I mean, who wants to be a momma's boy, right? Before I knew it, I just stopped talking about what was happening at school and bottling up all my emotions and pretending everything was fine. It felt easier at the time to just numb myself and not have to talk to anyone about it. That is what all the other guys seemed to do. It's what my dad did, too. I never saw him talk about anything hard he was going through or cry about what was happening in his life, so why would I?

After all, this is a huge part of what being cool means for men: being an emotionless robot. Getting upset or ruffled by something is the ultimate uncool move. And going home and crying to your mom about it—instant momma's boy loser status. So for us boys, this means masculinity is perpetually tied into acting emotionless and invulnerable.

For the record, this isn't even true. A 2018 study at the University of Arizona found that celebrities and public figures who were perceived as cool usually smiled more than others. That said, the study also showed that when two mixed martial artists faced one another at a press conference, the inexpressive one was deemed cooler. I can't help but think that it was men watching that press conference, being primed to watch an act of brutally tough violence, who perceived the blank-faced fighter as the cool guy, and it was women who thought celebrities who smiled more were cool. But back to school. . . .

The early messages I got weren't directly about how being a boy meant you needed to be assertive so much as they were about *not* getting upset or letting anything bother you. But how is that possible? Aren't human beings supposed to feel? Isn't that why they are called "feelings"? Yet to be accepted and deemed manly or cool, I had to kill off that part of myself. Literally.

One of my favorite authors, the late bell hooks (and don't worry, I didn't misspell her name. She went by a pen name and chose not to capitalize it because she wanted to be known for her ideas and not her identity), said that the first act of violence us males engage in is violence against ourselves. She called the act of suppressing your emotions and feelings just to be accepted "soul murder," because it kills off the very part of you that is the most alive.

It hurt when I felt I could not be who I really was in order to be cool, but still I forced myself to live by a set of rules that someone else invented so I could be liked and belong.

Gentle and caring? I'm a girl.

Loud and obnoxious? I'm hilarious (unless I'm trying too hard, in which case, never mind).

Smiling, happy, openhearted? I'm not mysterious enough. I'm too open and easy. Girls will never be interested in me and I'll always be in the friend zone.

Unbothered, unemotional, totally robotic? I'm chill. I'm interesting. I'm cool.

That last one's a real clincher. "Chill" has been turned into a virtue for men, as though outwardly reacting to something that's upsetting or hurtful makes someone weak. Sure, some people are melodramatic and make big, scary deals out of the tiniest things, but being blank-faced and monotone at all times isn't healthy either. Life isn't a poker game, where showing your feelings means giving everyone else the upper hand, yet we are raised thinking that's what happens. Like life is all one big game and we have to keep everything

"MOST ADULTS HAVE THE **ADVANTAGE** OF EDUCATION OVER CHILDREN, BUT **WHAT IS THE USE** OF AN EDUCATION IF THEY SHOW A BIG SMILE WHILE **HIDING NEGATIVE FEELINGS** DEEP INSIDE? CHILDREN DON'T USUALLY ACT IN SUCH A MANNER. IF THEY **FEEL ANGRY** WITH SOMEONE, THEY EXPRESS IT, AND THEN IT IS **FINISHED**. THEY CAN STILL PLAY WITH THAT PERSON THE FOLLOWING DAY."

THE DALAI LAMA

to ourselves and protect our feelings and emotions to avoid getting hurt.

But when you think about it, that's actually really sad. It means everything we do, we do out of fear—of rejection or judgment and a bunch of other things. Fear of being perceived as weak or less of a man. Fear that our masculinity will be challenged or even worse . . . questioned. At the end of the day, we've all been dealt cards in one way or another. And when things finally don't turn out your way—because let's face it, tough things happen to everyone, no matter how chill they are—it's going to be that much harder to navigate the hard experience and get the support you need and deserve if you are always the guy pretending to not have feelings.

The worst part is that eventually the pretending becomes the reality and we lose our ability to feel. It's like practicing something so much and getting so good at it, the action becomes second nature, like riding a bike, or perfected, like a baseball swing. It becomes muscle memory, but in this case, it's emotional memory. So when the time comes when our feelings or emotions would help us and we actually need them, we can't access them anymore because we've buried them down too deep.

All that being said, I believe that the people who act like they don't care still very much care. They feel pain, remember the times that everything went wrong, and hold it all in their hearts, just like the rest of us, but they are so detached from their feelings that they don't even realize that the pain from those memories is influencing their actions and is the reason they can't show anyone how they feel.

So my question for you is this: Would you rather be the guy working extra hard to look like nothing bothers him, or the dude who's open about his problems, to whom other boys can relate? Which person do you think is cooler?

FOOL'S GOLD

For me, some of the most lonely and painful moments from high school happened when those awful homecoming forms were handed out. If you haven't gotten to high school yet, the basic idea was that every kid was given a ballot and had to write down the names of the eight coolest, prettiest, most handsome, most charming kids in school, and they'd end up becoming the nominees for homecoming king and queen. If your name got written down by enough people, you made it onto the homecoming court. And that meant that you were popular. You were, as my friend Glennon Doyle writes in her book *Untamed*, "Golden."

Each year I sat there, secretly hoping *anyone* would see me as worthy enough to be on that list. To be golden. And yes, as embarrassing as it is, each year, I wrote in my own name. Not because I thought I would win, but because I just wanted someone—even if it was only the person who read and calculated the numbers—to see my name and know that someone thought I was worthy. That I was golden. That I was cool.

Each year, after I wasn't named to the homecoming court, I went through a mental list of what I could do differently, of how I could be different, to get nominated the next year. Maybe if I was a little funnier, a little louder, scored more goals, or broke more records on the track. Maybe if I was a little better looking or if my muscles were bigger. Maybe next year I could be golden, too, and then I'd finally meet everyone else's approval.

When I look back on it now, all I can think of are all the other kids who were forced to go through that torturous exercise and who were feeling exactly the same way I was. How many of us were looking at each other thinking the other was golden and we were not?

In a world where deep down lots of people just want to fit in, I wish we could realize that it takes true confidence to love ourselves and believe that we are enough. But I didn't understand that back then (it's even hard to understand it now), and instead I put on my armor each day, piece by piece, to create the facade of confidence that would make the loneliness a little more bearable.

All I wanted was to be enough. Because of that, I could never see that I already was.

LIKE, COMMENT, FOLLOW: THE LAND OF RYANS

One thing I've learned—and it hasn't been easy—is that no matter how cool I become, there will always be someone who is perceived to be cooler. Always. And in case you're wondering who a few of those people are for me: it's Tom Hardy and Jason Momoa, the actors who play Venom and Aquaman. Tom can do a million accents and transform his body for a role, and he portrayed the only Marvel superhero who has eaten someone's head onscreen. All that, and he overcame addiction to get where he is today. Jason is six foot four, built like a semitruck, and always outdoors going on some adventure, having a blast. I love that he can embody so many traditionally masculine traits while also staying in his joy. I definitely don't think I'm as cool as either of them. Or am I?

The thing is, neither of them probably thinks of himself as that cool. Everyone we consider cool have people *they* look up to and who they think are cooler. We like to think of ourselves on these different levels of cool, where some people are higher on the food chain than others. But what if we're all actually on the same level? What if fame, success, and swagger can never disguise the fact that we all have secret insecurities, and we're just doing our best to be as confident as we can?

> # "YOUR TIME IS LIMITED, SO DON'T WASTE IT LIVING SOMEONE ELSE'S LIFE."
>
>  STEVE JOBS
>
> ## FOUNDER OF APPLE

In high school, my Tom or Jason was a kid named Ryan. The unspoken rule at my school was that you were either a theater or art kid (and therefore pretty smart), or an athletic kid (who got by on sports). And then there was Ryan, who was both a standout athlete *and* an academic whiz. Not only that, but everyone liked him because he was kind and funny and had a smile that made you feel important. Ryan didn't gossip or bully, and never acted superior to the kids around him. People talked about him like he was a unicorn.

Of course, as a kid who had trouble with school and who also worked really hard to get in with the jocks, I was *so* jealous of Ryan. He was perfect. If my life in high school had been a movie, he would have been the guy in slow motion laughing with his friends who everyone looked at when he walked down the hallway. I would have been the guy with his hand up waiting for a high five that he didn't see and then hoping that no one witnessed me standing there like an idiot. Okay, maybe I'm being a bit dramatic, but there were days when I definitely felt like that!

Isn't it weird that because Ryan was so kind and awesome, I figured he'd never like me? Rather than take his good nature as an invitation to be his friend, I saw it as a reason to keep my distance from him for fear of rejection. I guess I thought if the nice guy didn't like me, then how could anyone?

Lately, when I think about Ryan, I wonder if he felt as cool as I thought he was. If there's one thing I've learned in my adult life, it's that sometimes the people who seem the coolest in public are the ones who are struggling the most in private.

This is an example of something called "impostor syndrome," which basically means that even people who have accomplished a lot and who are well-known or popular think of themselves as complete frauds. How could anyone like their movie/book/song/idea when there are so many other, better ones out there? What will happen when everyone realizes that they have no idea what they are doing? When will everyone realize they have been fooled?

That guy everyone thinks is the coolest usually struggles with the same insecurities that most of us do. And he's probably waiting for everyone to notice, because then he can relax a little instead of having to perform for everyone. Maybe all Ryan ever wanted to say to people was, "Stop acting like I'm so cool. I'm not."

When I was in high school, social media hadn't been invented yet, so Ryan was only popular in school. Today, all the Ryans in your life live in one very strange, fun, and confusing place: social media. Personally, I have a love-hate relationship with social media. On the one hand, I really enjoy the community I've built and think there's a lot of value in connecting with people on social media platforms. On the other hand, I recognize the challenges that social media presents. One of the biggest is the negative effect it can have on our confidence and self-esteem.

Lots of people my age who didn't grow up with social media like to blow it off like it doesn't matter, but statistics prove otherwise. A 2017 study about depression in teenagers published by *Clinical Psychological Science* found that after surveying over half a million eighth through twelfth graders—the number of them exhibiting high levels of depressive symptoms increased by 33 percent between 2010 and 2015—exactly the five-year period when smartphone ownership among young people became widespread.

Not only does social media provide one with a measuring stick for personal value—a literal number of friends and likes—but it gives you a nonstop parade/highlight reel of just how awesome everyone else's life is. You rarely get to hear about what a hard day someone has had, or how sad they are feeling. There are trends on social media apps that make you feel like you HAVE to do them or you risk being left behind, and if your videos aren't going viral or getting views it's easy to feel like there is something wrong with you.

If you want to build confidence, you can't always be comparing yourself to everyone else. You can look up to people you admire, sure, but trying to *be* them at the expense of being you is just a recipe for disaster. Take it from me, I've been

GUT CHECK

CLEAN YOUR FEED

If you're old enough to be on social media, next time you log on, unfollow anyone who doesn't bring you happiness, or to whom you compare yourself. If someone's pictures or videos only make you jealous or angry, unfollow them (or at the very least mute them). Clean your feed until it's only your friends and or people whose content you find truly interesting. Content that makes you feel good, inspired, or joyful.

there and done that and it didn't go well. There is a quote I love: "Comparison is the thief of joy." And it is. Because joy is innate; it comes from within. And like happiness, joy comes from being content with what you have. When we compare ourselves to others, we are literally robbing our souls of feeling the joy we deserve by saying that we aren't enough as we are. In a world where there will always be someone smarter, funnier, better looking, more athletic, or cooler than us, we have to find a way to be content and happy with what we have and who we are. And that will never happen if we look outward and compare ourselves to others. And for us, that means being very mindful that we aren't trying to be like other boys just to gain admittance to the boys' club.

> **"THE REASON WE STRUGGLE WITH INSECURITY IS BECAUSE WE COMPARE OUR BEHIND-THE-SCENES WITH EVERYONE ELSE'S HIGHLIGHT REEL."**
>
> **STEVEN FURTICK**
> AUTHOR AND PASTOR

WELCOME TO THE BOYS' CLUB

Most of the time the term "boys' club" means a male-dominated culture inside of an organization. It could be anything from a tree house to a sports team or a message board. But where the boys' club really exists is in our minds, and it's bigger than any walls could hold.

The boys' club is anywhere a bunch of boys gather and where we change our behavior if a girl comes in. It's when we talk about all the sexual things we claim to have done (which most of the time we haven't). It could be a mean inside joke about someone that we can laugh at, and then when that someone walks by, we laugh together and make everyone else feel like they aren't included. It's telling a story to a group of guys with the unspoken agreement that they won't tell anyone else, because that would be breaking the unwritten rules of what it means to be a guy.

In fact, it's a code. Some call it "the bro code" or "the guy code." Either way, everyone knows boys never tell or snitch on other boys, even if the thing the boy did or said was horrible. Now, obviously, no one ever taught us this officially, but it didn't have to be taught for us to learn it. It's not like we ever sit down with our buddies and say, "Okay, boys' club meeting. Invoke the oath of privacy." But we do feel it, like it was a set of rules we were taught in our sleep. But if there's no written rules for the boys' club, then how do we learn the rules we abide by? They have to come from somewhere, right? The answer is that most of the time, they're picked up from the influencers in our lives—from watching other guys in social settings and in family settings. There's a sense that if you want to be part of the crew, you've got to follow the rules—and if you have to ask what they are, you're probably going to be a buzzkill and won't be invited to the next meeting.

So what makes a boy valuable to the club? How do we get our name on the list? Who even decides who gets in or not? Sometimes it seems like the things we're into give us a head start—like what music, sports, or games we like. As boys and men, we bond over common interests as they make us feel like we're part of a special group of guys. And it doesn't matter what the thing is. It could be liking the same sports team, playing the same video game, or even being a part of the same online community or message board. Regardless of the thing that brings guys together, once you are finally in the group, your spot is never quite secure, which is why there is value in going along with whatever the other guys say.

When you don't have a secure spot, the last thing you want to do is challenge someone who can reject you. For those boys (and I have been that boy plenty of times) silence is the ultimate tool—we don't call out the words or behavior of another guy, especially if he's more popular than we are. We don't speak up when another boy does something cruel or says something horrible about someone else because speaking up would mean risking our membership in the club.

To speak up would be to reveal that we're not willing to put our principles on the line in the name of the boys' club—and would risk no longer being part of the crew. If we've got nothing else going for ourselves—if we're not popular or cool on our own—we sometimes feel like we have to do whatever it takes to stay on the inside. All it takes is bottling up our emotions and keeping our mouths shut. And guess what? While I try to not generalize too often, pretty much every boy who belongs to a group has done this. Yep, all of us.

But we are better than this!

Trying to bottle up your emotions and stay silent when you know you should speak up is just an awful way to live. Imagine your feelings are like a balloon. When you first get one, it's just this thin piece of rubber. Now pretend that every time someone hurts you, or you find yourself in a situation that doesn't feel right but you don't say anything, the balloon blows up a little. Well, if you don't ever let air out of the balloon (aka allowing yourself to feel your feelings or speaking up when something isn't right), the balloon will eventually fill up to the point that it pops. And when it does, it makes quite a loud noise, so loud it can scare you and the people around you.

For me, there has always been an easy way to tell if something is off or to know that what I'm doing (or what someone else is doing) is wrong: the knot in my stomach. Here's a moment where the gut check is the way to go—recognizing when something just doesn't *feel* right in your body. Throughout my life, I've always known right from wrong, but that doesn't mean I've listened. When I've tried to hold in the wrong instead of saying what's right, it feels like my gut is making a fist and it's pressing on my solar plexus. Sometimes it's even hard to breathe.

The problem is that once again, even when we feel those things, we convince ourselves that we have to push through it and ignore the undeniable voice inside ourselves, the voice that makes us human.

Unfortunately, the boys' club rewards us for silencing that inner voice. When I used to put someone else down (usually behind their back) or talk about a girl in class like she was an object and not a person (100 percent ALWAYS behind her back), I gained social currency and scored points with the other guys. The sad thing is that I would do it despite knowing how bad it was for my soul.

In the Bahá'í faith, we are told one of the worst things we could ever do is gossip because it is the root cause of disunity. It pits us against each other, and it's hurtful to our souls. Some of the worst pain in my life has been the result of other people saying bad things about me or pointing out my faults, yet for whatever reason, just to gain admittance to a club I don't even really want to be a part of, I have gone against my own beliefs and done the same just to feel accepted.

What I realize now looking back is that if I was feeling bad about participating, the reward I got from the group overpowered any guilt I had and pushed me to keep doing it. Other guys would laugh at what I said or invite me to hang out on the weekends. I could sit at the cool table at lunch or play video games with the guys after school. Whatever attention I received made me feel like I was cool, and that mattered more than being seen for who I really was—a deeply feeling kid who just wanted to be liked and accepted.

Sometimes, I wish I could go back and tell twelve-year-old Justin that he had everything he needed to be cool. That all the things that made him uncool then—acting, loving art, not drinking or doing drugs—are his superpowers today. Then again, he probably would've shrugged and said, "How does that help me? You want me to spend the next *six years* getting bullied, made fun of, and tied to the soccer goalpost just because someday I'll be awesome?"

He has a point. But honestly, if I could go back in time as adult me and tell him anything, I think it would be these two things:

1. Listen to your body. Trust your gut. It will never steer you wrong.

AND—

2. You . . . are . . . enough. And when you are enough you don't need to go against your own values to satisfy other guys who don't really care about you. So no matter how hard it is, do what you feel is right, deep down. Speak up when you hear something that rubs you the wrong way. Hang out with those kids YOU like but other people don't. Don't speak if you don't really have something to say, and don't jump if you don't want to.

You are enough already, and once you know it, everyone else will know it, too.

THE SENSITIVITY MUSCLE

So far, the rules of being cool for boys have rolled out like this:

- Act like the men who others look up to.
- If you're not cool, just go along with the other guys. Don't call them out or draw attention to yourself.
- Be big and be loud. And if you're not big, be the center of attention. Be impossible to ignore.
- Be chill.
- If you get hurt either emotionally or physically, suck it up and be a man. There's no crying in baseball.
- Get likes and follows on social media any way you can.
- If you don't know the answer, pretend you do.

- If someone tells you you're wrong, prove to them you're right.

What's the pattern here, besides the fact that half of these "rules" cancel the other ones out?

The pattern I see is numbness. None of these behaviors involve actually feeling something, other than a greedy desire to be cool. According to them, the most important part of being cool isn't just bottling up emotions, it's learning not to feel them entirely.

One of the ways this is especially harmful is in our friendships with other guys. If we're constantly worried about showing our emotions for fear of looking like a girl—or, even worse, policing other boys about not showing *their* emotions to make ourselves feel cool—then we're never going to make real, deep friendships. And while this idea exists that male friendships are all about video games, sports, where you sit in school, or who you sit by at lunch, the truth is that most guys want deeper friendships with each other; they just don't know how to have them.

When I try to make friends with another guy, it's always that first step—the call, the text—that's the hardest. I always feel like I have to test the waters, to make sure this guy actually cares about what I think and won't be put off by my honesty or use it as a way to make fun of me later. How sad is that—that my experience trying to be cool when I was younger made me uncomfortable *making friends*?

Now, this doesn't mean that every part of the friendship has to be filled with vulnerable conversations, because that would be exhausting! Friendships should also be fun and easygoing, but what's important is that we don't feel like that has to be the only way we communicate. We shouldn't be afraid to one day say to our friend, "You know what, man, I'm really struggling today" or "Someone said something and it really hurt me."

Real talk? Most of the time, that friend wants to tell you how *they're* feeling, too. People like empathy, kindness, and an awareness of emotion—in fact, they're drawn to these things, but they need permission to go there. By letting them know that showing up authentically is cool with you, it means that both of you can stop worrying about being cool and start being human.

Sensitivity isn't just something you have; it's something to work on. It's a muscle, in that it gets stronger and stronger every time you use it. And just like a muscle, if you don't it atrophies and gets weaker and weaker. Practicing your sensitivity can also involve some pain and stress, only instead of that resistance coming from your body, it's coming from other boys who may try to tease you or make you

GUT CHECK

OPEN UP

Do you have a friend whose opinion is important to you? Today, be real with that person. Tell them if you're feeling really happy about something, or if you're having a hard time. Call them just to tell them that you care about them and why. Ask them how they're really feeling and see if you can be truly honest with each other. It might be tough, but this is a good first workout of your sensitivity muscle.

feel less than for expressing your feelings. But the reward of not having to lock up your emotions, of being honest with yourself and developing friendships due to that honesty, is so worth it.

Get strong. Build your emotional muscles. Lift the weight of your feelings. Learn how to actually feel your feelings. It's not nearly as hard as trying to act cool, but in the long run, it's the coolest thing there is.

BREAKING IT DOWN

IN BOYS, COOLNESS IS ASSOCIATED WITH CONFIDENCE.

Feeling sure of yourself to the point of perfection is where our ideas of "cool" come from.

THE PROBLEM IS, MOST PEOPLE AREN'T CONFIDENT.

The coolness we often see guys performing on social media or at school is usually just a lot of theater. Everyone doubts themselves—it's how you confront those feelings that matters.

IT'S BETTER TO BE REAL THAN TO BE "CHILL."

Acting like nothing fazes you, or like you're emotionally numb, just makes you feel terrible in the long run and makes the people around you feel worse.

LET'S CANCEL OUR MEMBERSHIP TO THE BOYS' CLUB.

Defending cooler boys or staying quiet when they behave inappropriately is an easy way to a make yourself feel nauseous. Stop playing by the rules of the boys' club—and maybe start your own, where EVERYONE is welcome.

STRENGTHENING YOUR SENSITIVITY MUSCLE IS THE EASIEST WAY TO ACTUALLY BECOME "COOL."

When you work hard at being emotionally open and honest, you'll find that it gets easier. Once it becomes second nature, people will respect you for who you are—or they won't, in which case, life goes on. What matters is that you feel confident in being yourself, and when you are confident in yourself, you become a magnet, and suddenly everyone wants to be around you because you make THEM feel cool.

4

BOYS WILL BE
BIGGER

HEADS UP! This section of the book explores my experience with body image as a cisgender man. (Being cisgender means identifying with the sex you were assigned at birth.) If you're exploring or questioning your gender identity and any of this content makes you feel discomfort, please feel free to read only what's of value to you.

THE PERFECT BODY

"Dude, where are your abs?"

I looked up from the mirror at Matt and Sean, two boys I played club soccer with. Our team was taking part in a tournament out of town, and we had just gone for a dip in the motel hot tub. We were getting changed in the bathroom afterward when these guys started checking out their emerging abs in the mirror—and then they turned to twelve-year-old me and started laughing.

"What?" I said.

"Ha ha, you've got no abs, man," Sean said.

I looked in the mirror and saw that they were right. Sean and Matt had visible abs, and I had, you know, an average twelve-year-old stomach. But it wasn't just that—I also noticed that these guys were bigger and had hair growing in places I didn't. They were what I would eventually think of as "alpha males"—physically superior specimens in every way. They had chiseled athletic bodies, and even though I was athletic, too, I was skinnier than them, with thin and bony shoulders and arms.

"It's okay, man, one day you'll catch up," said Matt. "Or not!" Then they laughed. And I laughed, too, not wanting to seem too sensitive. To those guys, or any random adult watching us, it probably seemed like the most lighthearted teasing boys could engage in.

Of course, for me, it was like falling off a cliff. A knot formed deep in my ab-less stomach—a knot that, honestly, wouldn't leave me for years, and still pops up occasionally today. A dark, gross, twisted feeling that my body was wrong. That it wasn't enough. That it was a boy's body and not a man's body, which, according to the lessons I'd gathered from watching sports and movies and reading comic books, usually included sleeve-ripping biceps, broad shoulders, and, you guessed it, six-pack abs.

Before we get too deep into this chapter, I want to make something very clear: health and fitness are super important to me. It's a huge part of my identity as both a man and a human. Working out and being active brings me joy and is

"ANYBODY WHO'S GONE THROUGH PUBERTY KNOWS WHAT IT'S LIKE TO BE AN OUTCAST AND ALONE."

CHRIS PINE
ACTOR

something I will always love to do. Hitting the gym, getting a sweat on, pushing your body—these things can be really fun, and they're good for your overall health and your mind. Taking care of your body, or taking pride in your appearance, isn't a bad thing, but what I've learned over the years is that sometimes we want to work out for the wrong reasons, and that can be more harmful to our mental and emotional health than not working out in the first place.

The truth is that the messages boys get about their bodies aren't really about their health. It's not enough to be physically fit. Boys have to be big, strong, muscular, sexy, *hot*. This is where boys can develop poor relationships with their bodies, and mainstream masculinity can make us feel terrible about ourselves for not living up to an unrealistic standard of what a man's body is supposed to look like. And not only is that not fair to boys *or* their bodies, but it also creates shock waves of harm in their lives that leave everyone disappointed and upset.

These issues bother us for years, but we aren't really given the space to talk about it. Body image insecurities? No way, man. Only girls are insecure about their bodies! Well, I have news for you: body image insecurities don't just affect girls, they affect guys too, and these insecurities really start during puberty.

129

PUBERTY: WHEN A BOY'S BODY STARTS TO MATTER

For ages, boys have been told by teachers, parents, and practically the whole world that puberty is when they "become a man." Really, it feels a little more like finding out you're a werewolf. There's hair growing everywhere, your voice cracks and then gets deeper, your face breaks out (and sometimes so does your neck, your shoulders, your back, your chest, your butt—yup, even your butt), and you're suddenly distracted by sexual attraction to other people, which occasionally feels like you're becoming some kind of feral animal (you're not, but the way society views your sexuality can give that impression—don't worry, we'll get to sex in chapter six).

Unlike everyone else, I'm here to go a little deeper than the people in your inner circle might and tell you that puberty is normal and a process every single one of us goes through, even though it might feel like the loneliest and most awkward experience in the world. But if you want the unfiltered truth, here it is.

Puberty sucks.

It's not some chill, beautiful time in your life. It can be really rough. But the physical changes aren't really the hard part—what's rougher are the expectations that come with it.

The issue with the whole "becoming a man" thing is that it sets this hard line between boys and men. This leaves boys who don't experience puberty as quickly or as strongly as others wondering if there is something wrong with them and if they are going to stay little kids forever. Being a few months "behind" can feel like years! It also leaves those kids growing mustaches and standing a foot above their peers at ten years old feeling like they're freaks. More than anything, puberty causes us to compare ourselves to others, which, coupled with what we see on social media, can lead to a lot of fear and anxiety.

Maybe if we started recognizing puberty as a spectrum and talking about these changes as they come, we could reduce a bit of the awkwardness. Maybe we can even share pointers with each other as we're going through it—"Yeah, my face broke out really hard. Use this cream" or "I'm getting these random erections in class and it's super awkward!" If we could be less embarrassed about how our bodies are evolving and changing, if we would be willing to share our experience with other boys and pass down the information to the younger ones, then maybe it could be a little more bearable and less lonely. At the end of the day, puberty isn't

CHECK IN WITH YOUR BODY

Close your eyes and take a moment to acknowledge how your body feels right now, without shame or judgment. Have you been through any physical changes lately? If not, what are you hoping for as your body starts changing? Now open your eyes and either write or say out loud all the things you love about your body and what you are thankful for. Think of it like a little thank-you note, and remind yourself that even if you want your body to change, you are grateful for it and all the abilities it gives you.

a race; it's something we're all in together. We're all werewolves now!

Actually, now that I think about it . . . maybe the whole "wolves" thing is part of the problem. Society (and Hollywood) have had a habit of turning boys hitting puberty into these predatory animals—but we're not. We're not wolves; we're humans. And most of the time we don't feel like the predators; we feel like the prey!

ALPHAS AND BETAS

A totally "ripped dude" with huge bulging arms, a broad chest, and a neck like a tree trunk isn't a normal body. In fact, a "normal" body doesn't really exist. And yet when we go to the movies, or watch sports, or play video games, that is how we're told boys and men are supposed to look. Even if we're not told directly, it's communicated by the fact that those body types make up many of the male bodies we get to see. There's no chubby Avenger (well, Thor did get chubby in *Endgame*, which I appreciated because it showed him struggling with depression and eating his feelings, but it was exaggerated for laughs), and no one on *WWE Raw* has a "dad bod," so the question becomes, if you're not big and bulky or chiseled like a Greek god, are you even a bro, bro? Okay, no one really talks like that, but you get my point.

This is the difference between your body and *body image*. Your body is what it is—brown eyes, five feet tall, size nine feet, whatever you have. Body image is how we *perceive* our bodies—and a lot of that is how we think other people see our bodies. And for boys, the thought is that people have to see our bodies as dominant. Hard-core. The most jacked body in the pack.

"LOOK, IT'S NOT THAT **HARD.** ALL YOU NEED TO DO IS **LIFT WEIGHTS** SIX DAYS A WEEK...DON'T EAT ANYTHING AFTER SEVEN P.M., **DON'T EAT** ANY CARBS OR SUGAR AT ALL, IN FACT JUST **DON'T EAT** ANYTHING YOU LIKE...RUN THREE MILES A DAY, AND HAVE A STUDIO **PAY** FOR THE WHOLE THING...**I DON'T KNOW WHY** EVERYONE'S NOT DOING THIS."

ROB McELHENNEY

IT'S ALWAYS SUNNY IN PHILADELPHIA ACTOR, ON HOW HE WENT FROM CHUBBY TO TRADITIONALLY BUFF

This is where the whole alpha/beta idea comes into play. This is a concept that has picked up steam over the years, especially on the internet, from men who claim that the world is being "feminized," which they believe goes against nature.

The basic idea is that among animals like wolves, there are alpha males—dominant, powerful leaders with the bodies and attitudes with which to rule over other members of the species—and beta males—weaker, ineffectual males who follow along because they're not big or strong enough to take care of themselves or defend the pack. Guys like to use this idea because it creates a hard line in the sand to be on either side of and gives them permission to judge people—themselves included—and treat them differently depending on which side of the line they fall. And usually, when someone's using the alpha/beta concept, they think of themselves as an alpha and are putting down someone else by calling them a beta (that's interesting, isn't it? I smell a lot of insecurity that no one is talking about here).

Here's the thing: the alpha/beta rule is super flawed. According to a fascinating article titled "Do Alpha Males and Females Actually Exist?" author Eric Devaney describes that scientifically, the term "alpha" refers to an individual with the highest rank in a social group. And in nature, that boils down to one thing: sex. The alpha male gets the first chance to mate with the females, not to mention first dibs on food, grooming, whatever.

Like I said before, there's a whole chapter later about sex, so I'm not going to get too deep into that now. But here's what I will say: molding your body into a weapon or a specific shape for the sake being the most powerful so you can have the most sex feels ridiculous. It immediately assumes that guys have nothing but sex on their minds and that it's the only thing that makes us men.

Also, why are we comparing ourselves to animals? Animals have only one social hierarchy (which is the way that they organize themselves)—violence. If you can beat up or kill any threat, you're the dominant animal, you're the alpha. But humans have a bunch of social hierarchies— strength, intelligence, social skills, etc. So an alpha on the basketball court might be a beta in the classroom. Without these other social hierarchies, we don't really have society as we know it.

So while many guys may think of themselves as alphas all they want, all they're saying is that they think that they're entitled to dominate everyone else, which won't

DEBUNKED

THE ALPHA WOLF

Biology lesson: turns out the idea of the alpha wolf in nature isn't even real. In his 1970 book *The Wolf: The Ecology and Behavior of an Endangered Species*, Dr. L. David Mech observed that the scientists studying these "alpha wolves" were doing so in captivity—where wolves behave differently than they do in the wild because they're surrounded by all these humans prodding them and seeing their responses. To put it another way, imagine a bunch of aliens kept you and some of your friends in a cage and poked you with a stick over and over . . . and then built a whole philosophy around whoever acted like the angriest, biggest human of them all. Feels kind of silly, doesn't it?

benefit you after a while. That doesn't sound like a great way to make friends and allies, does it? At least not friends who aren't waiting for a chance to take you down so THEY can become the alpha. What goes around ALWAYS comes around.

Besides, it's well known that wolves work best in packs. These are animals with a complex social hierarchy, who live in family units, where the alpha male and female are just the mom and dad. Worrying about being the alpha wolf misses a vital point—that alone, you're inherently weaker.

The same is true about real life. Being an alpha physically only gets you so far—and when you find yourself up against other men who have been focusing on their mental and emotional health and their character, you'll feel less like an alpha and more like one of those guys you probably made fun of or called a beta. It's the circle of life.

THE SHAPE OF FEAR

In the first chapter, we talked a lot about how much of masculine "bravery" is based on taking physical risks and overcoming fear. This is also true with the idea of having an "alpha" body. The need to be the leader of the pack, all the silly wolf imagery—it's about fearing violence. In our modern world of endless social media feeds and daily tragedies thanks to a twenty-four-hour news cycle brought to you by companies that profit off our fear, so many humans around the world are living in a perpetual state of it.

Along with that fear is a deep and hidden fear-based belief system that many men live by that says that as men we have to be strong enough to defend ourselves and protect the ones we love. This is a rational fear for many men who deep down feel helpless and defenseless every day. Some of them even believe they can't protect themselves, their things, the people they care about, unless they turn their bodies into a weapon that is strong enough to fight back. And if their bodies aren't strong enough, and sometimes even if they are, they feel they need to carry a weapon. What happens if the terrible thing comes, or they or someone they love is threatened and they're not prepared or too much of a "beta" to stop it?

Well, this fear translates into an overcompensation that is known as the "hero complex." In some ways being strong enough to protect yourself and those around you is a good thing. But again, humans have different hierarchies. Sometimes hard things show up—tragedy, depression, shame, confusion—that no amount of muscle or fight training can stop. And if we live our lives bulking up or turning our bodies into weapons in fear, instead of learning how to deal with our emotions, then we never actually grow in the way that will matter in the end. Sure, we may be buff or carry a gun, but we're still in pain and confused about how we feel. And what's the point of being jacked if you're also completely out of touch with the very parts of you that make you human?

THE SHAME GAME

Body-shaming is probably the most common form of bullying among young boys because it's an easy way to put someone else down to make yourself feel better. Sound familiar? According to a recent survey, 94 percent of all teenage girls and 64 percent of all teenage boys have been body-shamed at some point in their lives. Just like I was that day with my friends Sean and Matt. That's way too much, if you ask me. And it makes me wonder if the outside messages we're receiving are not only making us critical of ourselves, but critical of others. Like if we have to follow the rules of being buff, or hot, or attractive, and if we are consuming media that reinforces that idea as well, then it's obvious that we will be judging ourselves and everyone else, too. And with body-shaming, a kid who is teasing you doesn't need to be clever, or cruel, or thoughtful. Our bodies are right there in the open. "You're fat/skinny/short/tall/disabled, and I'm not." Simple.

Well, except for one thing: the *and I'm not* part. People who body-shame are rarely super confident in their own bodies. They often have someone who rips on them. It can be a thing that most people wouldn't even notice—the shape of their eyes, or their teeth, or the way they walk— but in their mind, that thing makes them feel ugly and not enough. This doesn't excuse their hurtful behavior of putting someone else down just to lift themselves up, but it's important to remember that they are probably also feeling insecure just like you are.

I should know—I was both a victim of bullying *and* I was someone who bullied. When my family moved from LA to Oregon, I had no friends, and my Jewish-Italian features, especially my "Roman nose" and massive eyebrows, stuck out in our little town. Even though I was a skinny kid, I subconsciously knew I could try to prove my worth as the new kid through anything sports-related. But when I was feeling the most insecure, I took it one step further—and started drawing attention to someone else's body.

I'll never forget this one awful moment, a desperate attempt to be accepted during a game of kickball in PE. A boy who was overweight stood up to the plate, and I shouted from the outfield, "Let's go, fat-ass!" and laughed at my own joke. Even at ten years old, I had absorbed enough messaging to believe that if I wanted to feel like an alpha, I should automatically prey on someone else.

Later that day, a teacher called me out on my behavior. The minute she made me consider what I'd done, I was ashamed of myself, and that comment became one of those moments I'll always regret. Not only was it cruel and hurtful to the kid I directed it to, it also made me feel awful. I learned an important lesson that day: when it comes to body-shaming, there are no winners. When you engage in that behavior, everyone loses.

The truth is that though men and boys have absorbed

> ## "IT'S NOT THE SIZE OF A MAN, BUT THE SIZE OF HIS HEART, THAT MATTERS."
> ### EVANDER HOLYFIELD
> **FORMER HEAVYWEIGHT CHAMPION**

tons of harmful messages about how big, muscular, or traditionally attractive we are, we're not alone in the race. Far from it.

Everything men and boys are dealing with, women and girls have had to deal with for much longer, and with much harsher standards. That's because long before the feminist movement championed the idea that women's feelings were worth taking into account, women were expected to do everything with the goal of marrying a man. It was the reverse "alpha" scenario—if women made themselves obedient enough, maybe an alpha would pick them and stay with them. As a result, women were expected to adhere to every changing trend in body type—thinner, thicker, taller, shorter, bigger, smaller, more makeup, no makeup. Even then, it never ends for women—if they're too sexy, they can't be smart and they must be "sluts;" if they're not sexy enough, they're "plain" or "prudes." If they are too smart or powerful, they are "bossy." And it's important to note that in many other cultures, the unfair expectations of women are way more extreme.

It's not that boys somehow have it better than girls, only that girls feel it more acutely. According to a 2015 study, 25 percent of boys in the United States were concerned

FEMINISM?

Feminism is the belief that women of every race, ethnicity, and religion—no matter who they love, or how they express their gender—should be considered equals to men in all things. Men and women shouldn't be judged or treated differently from one another. It's that simple.

about looking lean and muscular or having more defined muscles. But a similar study in 2006 showed by age thirteen, 50 percent of all girls were unhappy with their bodies, and 80 percent of girls feared getting fat.

These messages have led to women having terrible feelings about their bodies over the years and have driven many of them toward harmful behaviors or eating disorders like anorexia (starving oneself) or bulimia (making oneself throw up after eating in order to stay a certain weight). There is no "out," either—no "dad bod" for women to feel good about even if it doesn't conform to typical standards. If a man is rich and successful but not traditionally attractive, he's just winning; if a woman is the same, her body or looks are something she overcame to become successful, like she somehow did well *despite* not being traditionally attractive.

I bring all this up for three reasons. First, body issues aren't something that either men or women own—it's something we share. While it's important that we explore body image issues, we can't act as though boys' experiences are more important than girls' experiences. We are truly all in this together. Second, it's important for men to understand that at times body image issues in boys were overlooked because this was considered a "girls' problem," and because boys aren't allowed to be insecure or have any sort of feelings about their bodies aside from confidence.

And third, as the title of this book suggests, boys are humans—just like girls (as well as nonbinary and trans kids), who have put up with this pressure and judgment from the world for far longer than us. We should look to women to help us understand how to overcome these issues and meet their experience with compassion and empathy. After all, it's because of the "male gaze" (the way men see women) that women have felt the pressure to look a certain way in the first place. In fact, the "male gaze" creates the pressure for boys to feel and look a certain way, too. This is just another example of how these traditional ideas of masculinity aren't helping anyone.

GENDER?

When you're born, your "sex" is determined by whether you have a penis (male) or a vagina (female) or both (intersex). "Gender" is one of the ways people express their identity. "Gender roles"—ideas of what behaviors are right for boys and girls—have been around a long time and affect us a lot more than we think.

There's also the issue of certain bodily functions somehow being seen as gross just because they happen to girls. I'm thinking specifically of periods—since forever, girls have had their totally normal, natural menstrual cycles portrayed as somehow disgusting. But again, we have to ask ourselves: Why? Is it because there's blood? Plenty of boys watch action and horror movies full of gore. I mean, if a boy gets bloody, it's seen as cool! If I had to guess, the real issue is that boys have been told over and over that girls' bodies are meant solely for their pleasure. So anything that doesn't seem pretty or sexy becomes kind of gross.

Think of it this way: Why is it okay for a boy to fart or

smell up the bathroom with a big crap, but if a girl did the same thing, she would be gross?

We have double standards for girls and boys, and anything we don't understand, we push away or make fun of because it makes us uncomfortable. So because boys aren't really taught what a period is or how painful it can be for many girls, women, nonbinary, and trans people, we just avoid it like the plague and make fun of what they're going through. I want to set the record straight: making someone else feel like they're somehow dirty or disgusting for something like having a period is one of the meanest things we could ever do.

Let's stop obsessing over bodies in general and start looking at each other as whole people instead.

A THOUGHT OR TWO ON GENDER

I believe that before we are anything we are spiritual beings first. As I said before, I have a body, but I am not my body. And in the same context: I have a gender, but I am not my gender. From a spiritual perspective it could be argued that the soul has no gender attached to it. I try to think of it like this: if my body is a lamp, my soul is the light within the lamp making it glow. But I am not the lamp, I am the light within it.

I see so much pain, frustration, and anger surrounding the subject of gender these days, and many people are feeling the need to control other people's bodies, as if how someone else expresses their gender identity is a threat to their very existence. Why are we so focused on the lamp and not the light? If you are gender nonconforming or trans, I just want to say it must be so hard when your identity is debated and disregarded by other people. I see you and have so much compassion for your experience.

However, if you are someone who feels threatened or uncomfortable by someone else's gender identity, let's use some of what we've learned in previous chapters, dig deep, and find out why! In my opinion, being a good human means learning to love and care about one another, even when we don't quite understand someone else's experience. So let's focus on our own light first and not worry about other people's lamps.

My friend the author and poet Alok Vaid-Menon said it perfectly when they were a guest on my podcast: "We must start to value compassion over comprehension. We shouldn't have to understand someone to have compassion for them." I wish everyone could take this sentiment to heart, because the world would be so much kinder if we did.

ALL RIGHT, LET'S GET EMBARRASSING

I'm going to tell you guys a story. It's straight-up mortifying, but I'm going to be brave here because I think it's important to talk about the things that make us uncomfortable. It's kind of funny, so don't worry about laughing. But if you laugh, do me a favor: when it's over, ask yourself *why* you laughed.

Okay. Deep breath. Here goes:

When I was twelve, I got erections all the time. Which, by the way, is completely NORMAL. That's right; if you didn't already know, boys start getting erections when they are born. In fact, some say it can happen in the womb. It's not even sexual; it's just part of being a boy. When we hit puberty, and as our bodies start producing more testosterone, involuntary erections start to happen more often, especially in the morning (some call this "morning wood").

The crazy thing is when I got erections, more than half the time I wasn't even thinking *about* something sexual. I'd just be sitting in the car, or class, and BOOM. Sometimes, I didn't notice it happening, and other times it would happen just before the bell rang, which is the worst time ever for a boner to appear. All that to say, if and when you start getting erections all the time, just know it's a sign of sexual

149

and reproductive health and that your body is healthy and working the way it was designed to. It shouldn't be an embarrassing or shameful thing. It happens to all of us. It's only embarrassing because we don't talk about it, and anything we don't talk about then becomes not normal . . . even when it's completely normal.

Okay, back to my story. One time I went to the mall with my family. My aunt was visiting us from out of town and came along for the ride. The drive to the mall was about thirty minutes from our house, and I should have known better, but back then whenever I was sitting for long periods of time "little Justin" would get tired of sitting and decide to stand (get it?). When we arrived in the parking lot and all piled out of the car, I didn't realize I had an erection, so I didn't get to tuck it up into my underwear like I normally did. As I stepped out of the car, my aunt pointed at my shorts and asked me what I had put in my pocket, because whatever it was, "it sure wasn't very funny."

I looked down and cringed. Cue the longest, most awkward silence of my life, followed by my aunt saying something like, "Oh, okay! Okay, let's go, let's go!" Yeah, she thought I had put something in my pants to make a boner joke when in reality she just caught me having an actual boner.

Naturally, I spent the day looking for a bottomless pit to jump into, I was so humiliated.

You might be thinking, *Uh, Justin . . . why are you telling us this?*

Well, first off, being vulnerable with each other can help us get past any hang-ups or worries about embarrassment we might have about our bodies. If I share an embarrassing moment in my life, you feel more comfortable talking about your embarrassing moment with someone else. Basically, the sooner we break down the walls that keep us feeling ashamed and humiliated about our bodies, the more we're able to trust each other, and that's no small thing. This is how we make taboo topics not taboo anymore—by talking about them!

Second, if you've been in a similar situation, I hope my story makes you feel less alone. Did your body ever do something unexpected, and you were mortified by it? Good—it's normal! And it shouldn't have to feel like it's the end of the world.

Lastly, it's time we confront an important part of male body issues. And I want you to be ready for it. Because if you're like the confused, body-negative boy I was, no one else has made you ready for it. Maybe because many adults are still embarrassed about THEIR bodies, but probably because no one ever talked to them about it either.

THE BIG "BIG"

We've had a lot of real talk in this book so far. I've been vulnerable with you, and maybe you've felt a little vulnerable with me. Only four chapters in, and we've come a long way.

SO . . . let's talk about penises.

This is a sensitive subject, because, well. . . our penises are really sensitive. (Okay, sorry, I promise that'll be my only bad joke in this section.) But when we're talking about our bodies and body image with men, we can't *not* talk about this, given how much emphasis is put on it for boys going through puberty, and maybe even more so after puberty.

The message we receive from magazines, music, and movies is that a man's penis should be big and able to get hard whenever he wants it to. It should be ready for sex at a moment's notice and should be as long and thick, if not more so, than the penises of all the other boys around you. In fact, it's even better if it's bigger than anyone else's (as if that's in anyone's control). There's even a popular term, "big dick energy," which roughly means "exuding confidence

Try this body-positive exercise every day for a week:

- In the morning, the first time you look in the mirror, repeat after me: "I *have* this body, but this body doesn't define me."
- Then find one part of your body you like and speak it out loud. "I love my eyes."
- Finally, hold your hand over your heart and say, "You are enough." If that makes you feel uncomfortable, that's okay. That can happen when you try something new.

or security." The idea is that if you have a penis that isn't huge, you'll be insecure or sensitive, and therefore come off as weak and no one will be attracted to you. (The flip side of this is that if you do have a large penis, people assume you'll automatically be confident, which is not the case either.)

But that sensitivity and insecurity doesn't come from the size of your penis. It comes from all of these other people TALKING about the size of your penis or the size it should be! Boys probably wouldn't care that much about penis size if the whole world wasn't always telling them that it matters.

Having a penis isn't a contest, because there's really no one to fight against, and there's no winner at the end of the day. But sometimes it feels like the outside world wants to make it one. With "big dick energy," suddenly not just our masculinity but our whole outlook on life is being related to the size of our penises.

At the same time, when a man is overly concerned with masculinity, or worries about being seen as scared or weak in front of other men, they're told they are taking part in a "dick-measuring contest." As though we're pitiful for even caring about penis size. One minute, we should be worried about our penises; the next, we're being stupid for worrying.

A popular concept is that sexual partners prefer men with huge penises, because they'll be better at sex. But like so many of boys' body image issues, the emphasis on penis size really comes from boys trying to be better than other boys. As an adult who has two kids and therefore has had sex at least twice in his life (sorry—another terrible joke), and who also has plenty of friends who have slept with men, I can assure you that penis size isn't a big deal at all. Intimacy, honesty, connection, a desire to learn—these are the things that people are usually most impressed by when it comes to a sexual partner. Also, I have never met a single person who has stayed with a partner just because of sex or penis size. Sure, some partners might be focused on size, but most aren't eyeing a guy's crotch to determine if they have a personal, emotional, and spiritual connection with the person.

All penises look different. Some are bigger, some are smaller. Some are circumcised, and some are not. Your penis will probably change with puberty—hair will grow around it, your testicles might hang lower. But at the end of the day, it's a functional part of your body, like your nose or ears. Unless you're scared that there's something medically wrong with your body, time spent worrying about the state of your penis is time wasted. And just remember, many guys with a normal-sized penis are also thinking their penis might not be big enough, too. That's why two of the top ten Google searches around sex is "how to measure a penis?" and "how to get a bigger penis."

So let me just give it to you straight. There will always be a guy with a bigger penis than you. AND there will always be someone with a smaller penis than you. Your life will not be better or worse because of the size of your penis, but the size of your heart . . . now that makes all the difference in the world.

HOW BIG IS BIG ENOUGH?

Here's a fun fact I learned from Dr. Roberto Olivardia, a clinical psychologist I've spoken to on my web series *Man Enough*. When the toy G.I. Joe was first introduced in 1964, if his size had been true to life, he would have stood five feet, ten inches tall with a thirty-one-inch waist, a forty-one-inch chest, and twelve-inch biceps. Strong and muscular, yes, but still a very achievable male body. Flash forward to 2002: G.I. Joe was still five feet ten, but his waist had shrunk to twenty-eight inches, his chest had ballooned to fifty inches, and his biceps were now twenty-two inches—close to the size of his waist. If this Joe were a real human, he would be unable to touch his own shoulder, let alone complete a special ops mission and save the planet. Can you imagine G.I. Joe parachuting in to stop a bomb from detonating, except he can't reach behind his back to get the tool from his belt because his biceps have basically given him T. rex arms?

The truth is that the makers of G.I. Joe aren't just trying to sell us a body type that's overblown or extreme in one direction or another—they are selling us a body type that is literally *unrealistic*. And it goes to show that our understanding of "masculine" bodies isn't always about wanting to look

THE WHY LADDER

The Why Ladder is a simple way to figure out the hidden feelings behind something you're doing or want to do. For example, with your body: you want to go to the gym. Why? To work out and get strong. Why? Because being strong is important to you. Why? Is it a hero complex? Because you want to impress someone? Because you are afraid of a classmate at school? Climbing the Why Ladder will help you get to the core of what you're actually worried about, rather than get caught up in the lessons you've been taught by outside influences. And knowing your *why* can help you make decisions from a place of strength instead of from a place of fear.

healthy, or even good. Sometimes, it's about looking the way we *think* men are supposed to look. But that image can get distorted in our minds and rarely has its roots in reality. And just like the wind blows, that expectation can change constantly, depending on the influences around us.

The lesson here: there's *always* going to be a body type different from yours. The perfect body exists only in your mind—*something* will always make your body, or the bodies of men around you, imperfect. And that's because our idea of the perfect body isn't real. It's a mishmash of messages that the media and our less-than-reliable influencers have branded into our minds. Just think about all those super-ripped guys on the covers of magazines or the actors in superhero movies. Those dudes are constantly working on getting their bodies to be perfect for a single moment that can be captured on camera . . . not forever. They are getting paid to break their bodies down as a full-time job, and then once that job is over, they always go back to looking like your average guy.

Having a perfect body is also a target that will forever keep moving because there will always be room to improve. And so long as there is someone with a "better" body than yours (and remember that what makes a body "better" or "ideal" is constantly changing, too), you will never be satisfied unless you can find peace and contentment with the body you currently have.

Remember what I said about impostor syndrome when it comes to being cool? Well, when it comes to beating ourselves up about our bodies, I think a lot of it comes down to a mix of impostor syndrome and some kind of pain we're trying to avoid at all costs. But when pain drives our actions, there is no amount of success that can heal it. For instance, if you're being bullied for being skinny and get really jacked in response to that, you'll still never feel big enough. Healing that kind of pain can only be done if you run toward it instead of away from it.

GOOD NEWS, BAD NEWS

Right now, your body might be changing pretty rapidly. Or maybe it's not, and it feels like everyone else's is, but you're not growing as fast. Well, I have good news and bad news. Bad: your body's going to keep changing, and you may never look exactly like how you wish you would. To this day, when I look in the mirror, the first place my eyes go is to my shoulders; if they don't fill out a T-shirt then I oftentimes won't even wear it. When I was twelve, I used to wear two T-shirts at once to make my shoulders look bigger than they were because I was always very aware of how narrow my shoulders were in comparison to some of the other guys', especially the older, popular ones. But if I get honest with myself, I know that my shoulders could be six feet wide, and it wouldn't be enough because as a boy I wasn't enough.

Here's the good news: you are not your body! I keep saying this because it's so darn important, so let me say it again. You *have* a body, but there is so much more to you than the lamp the light is contained in. Your body is yours. It's something you own—in fact, it may be the *only* thing you own, and the beauty is you never even had to buy it. It was a gift. And just like material possessions, if we aren't thankful for them and are always looking for something better, then we are never really happy with what we have. Happiness starts with contentment.

But how do we get out of our heads and focus less on body image to find that contentment? Step one is definitely confronting it and talking it out. The more we believe in this idea of "alphas" and being jacked or looking cool, the deeper a hole we dig for ourselves. The more we compare ourselves to this unrealistic ideal the more unhappy we become.

So let's start talking about what we LOVE about our bodies. When we look at ourselves in the mirror, let's try to appreciate what we see. Think about what parts of our bodies we think are unique and special. Let's celebrate our badonkin' booties and crazy weird feet! Feeling comfortable in our own skin starts with accepting and loving that skin, and once we are comfortable, hopefully we can give others the freedom to be comfortable in theirs.

BREAKING IT DOWN

IT'S OKAY FOR PUBERTY TO BE COMPLICATED.

Puberty may feel like it comes "early" or "late"—but regardless of when it comes, it's always a complicated time, and an experience every grown person on the planet has experienced.

YOUR BODY AND BODY IMAGE ARE DIFFERENT THINGS.

How you view your body or think your body is perceived versus how your body actually is can be two very different things.

THE "ALPHA MALE" IS A MYTH.

The "ideal" male body and the "alpha male" are both unrealistic. It's not the size of our penises or biceps that matter, but the size of our hearts.

MUCH OF OUR BODY IMAGE IS DRIVEN BY FEAR.

It's easy to be worried that we're not big and strong enough to protect ourselves or the ones we love. But strength comes in many forms, and oftentimes the biggest and strongest men in the room feel like they are the weakest. Using the Why Ladder can help us make better decisions, especially when it comes to our bodies.

WE HAVE A BODY, BUT WE ARE NOT DEFINED BY OUR BODIES.

While our bodies are something we have, they are only one aspect of who we are. We can't take our bodies with us when we die. They are like the lamp that contains the light. Let's show up for ourselves and each other and be the people we want to be, regardless of shape or size.

5

BOYS WILL BE
BOYS

HAVES AND HAVE NOTS: HOW BOYS BENEFIT FROM PRIVILEGE

Right now, "privilege" is a loaded word. You might have heard it used with a lot of anger, sarcasm, or even tears behind it. But what does privilege actually mean when we talk about everyday life as a boy?

Privilege is when the world treats certain people differently than others based on their being part of a group that society deems of greater worth. Or to put it another way, it's that being part of the biggest group, or the most common group—in America, like being a white male—means you get treated better than people who aren't white males, partly because society was built on rules that benefit them.

The thing about privilege is that it's not always about what you experience; it's often about what you *don't* experience. If you're part of a privileged group, your standard for normal is different than it is for less-privileged folks. And there are all different kinds of privilege; one you might have heard about is white privilege (we'll talk about that, too). But male privilege is a very real thing and needs to be addressed. There's even able-bodied privilege, which I'll admit I didn't even learn or think about (because I didn't have to) until recently. And just the fact that I didn't know about it, well, that's a perfect example of privilege.

When we say someone is privileged, a lot of people think it means that person has a lot of money or that their life is easy. Let's say you met a boy who was born into a family of billionaires. He asks you why you don't have the new Xbox and you explain that your family doesn't have the money to just buy you whatever you want. Then he says, "Just buy them with your credit card—what's the big deal?" Well, that billionaire boy has never known a life without money or can't imagine not being able to have what he wants. The idea that you can't buy an Xbox is almost impossible for him to understand. Just the fact that he doesn't understand is privilege, because he can literally afford to not understand it. Does that make sense? In other words, Boy Billionaire can't understand your life, because things have always been easier for him in the area of money. And guess what? It's not his fault. He was born into a family with money. Boy Billionaire isn't trying to be mean to you; he just doesn't understand your life.

So many of us live this way, even if we don't know it. And if we're being honest, one of the biggest groups that have privilege are boys born into male bodies. Checking our privilege is about building empathy and about understanding other people's experiences, but more than understanding it's about having compassion for other people and being willing to listen to their stories—and believe them.

So just keep in mind that some of this might be difficult to hear and you might at first find a part of your body tensing up, like you want to defend yourself. If that happens, try to take a breath and remember that this is NOT an attack on you and no one is saying you are bad because you have privilege. It's a challenge to see if we can be courageous enough to own our privilege and be willing to use it to make the world a better and safer place for everyone.

Another thing to keep in mind: I have a few different kinds of privilege. As I said before, I'm a man. I'm white. I'm heterosexual. I'm able-bodied. That means a good portion of this chapter is going to come from that experience, since it's the one that I know best. But it doesn't mean that I have the last word on any of this stuff, because as I've said before, I'm still learning and growing as a human. Also, if you don't share any of the traits I listed above or your experiences are different from mine, it's okay. We're still far more alike than we are different.

MALE PRIVILEGE: WHAT WE NEVER HAVE TO DEAL WITH

In middle school, I, along with my guy friends, liked to snap girls' bras—basically we would run up behind girls when they weren't looking, yank their bra straps, and let them snap back. We did this almost every day, and I would always do it to the girls I had crushes on. There was something about touching part of a bra—even when I didn't have permission—that was so exhilarating to me. It was almost like eating a forbidden fruit because I was touching a very private part of a girl's clothing that was touching her boobs.

So in my mind, because I wasn't touching her actual breasts, I didn't see anything wrong with it, and neither did the other boys.

But yeah, it was wrong. Looking back, even if sometimes the girls would laugh, I wonder how much that actually hurt, both physically and emotionally—especially if you'd just started wearing a bra and were feeling self-conscious about it. At the time, though, I thought it was hilarious.

Gross.

There are so many layers of male privilege here. We thought we could touch these girls any way we wanted to, and never thought about their feelings—because we never had to. We never considered that having your bra strap snapped into your back might sting like crazy—because we never had to wear bras! And worst of all, we never worried about getting detention or having to publicly apologize for our actions—because we never had to! It was just a game that we started on the playground without the girls' consent. No big deal. Boys will be boys, right?

Man, is there any more privileged statement in the world than "boys will be boys"? By now, we've talked about this phrase enough to do a deep dive into what it really means. At the end of the day, it's a catchall, a way to avoid taking responsibility for one's actions, or to keep us from ever taking someone else's feelings into account. "Boys will be boys" is basically giving boys (and men) a hall pass for life by saying "You can't change how they behave; it's biology."

But is it? And who decided this? You guessed it . . . men. Because society has been organized so that men are perceived as being entitled to whatever they want. Because we live in a patriarchal culture that thrives off men controlling the majority of power in the world and normalizing dominance over one another to possess it. . . . That's just the way it is, right?

Male privilege shouldn't mean boys are allowed to impose the rules they like and break the ones they don't.

PATRIARCHY?

Patriarchy is a system or society in which men are always placed at the top and hold the most power. When someone talks about "the patriarchy," they are talking about the parts of society, and the people in it, who consciously or unconsciously give men more privilege and power.

But we'd be lying if we acted like boys don't get away with things because everyone assumes we are wired to push and even defy boundaries.

I think of privilege like a hurdle race. First of all, in a very literal sense, I am privileged to even be on the track, running that race, because a person in a wheelchair could not participate in that kind of race. So, right off the bat, that's able-bodied privilege. Does that mean that I didn't train my butt off? No, it simply means that I have an opportunity and advantage that's not available to everyone.

More important, even though we're all running the race on the same track, we each have our own sets of hurdles, or barriers, on the way to the finish line. As a white male,

GUT CHECK

THE PYRAMID SYSTEM

Generally speaking, those at the top of the pyramid have the most power and tend to be unaware of the experiences of those at the bottom. Those at the top typically make all the decisions that affect the entire pyramid, which results in the creation of rules, laws, and systems that benefit them. Do you think this is the best way for society to be organized? Write down all the ways you think the world would look if the pyramid didn't exist or looked different? How might things change for the better?

I don't have as many hurdles as others do—the hurdles of how society treats women, nonbinary, and trans people; the hurdles of race that affect Black, Latinx, Brown, AAPI, and Indigenous people; the hurdles of where I'm from and economic systems being organized to make my life harder; the hurdles of my sexuality being taboo or blasphemous for a huge portion of people.

Now that doesn't mean that I won't have hurdles—that there isn't struggle, that I am not working hard—it just means that my gender and skin color will never throw an obstacle in my path. But privilege or not, I still need to train my butt off and run my race. My lane still has hurdles that I have to jump over, but other people have more hurdles than I do, and some of them are higher and harder to clear.

So if you're like me, a person with more than one type of privilege, you might think, *Wait, I'm supposed to see something that's* not *happening to me? How do I do that?* I get it. It's easy to think of these things as totally invisible. But once you start becoming aware of your own privilege, you'll start having more empathy with those who aren't privileged in the same way. And once you start having empathy toward other people and seeing things from their point of view, you'll find that privilege isn't as invisible as you think. In fact, maybe it's standing right in front of you—you just didn't notice it until now.

HEY, HE LOOKS LIKE ME!

How did we get here? The answer to this question is complicated, but the long and short of it is: white men throughout history did their damnedest to claim and protect their power. They thought that without it, they'd lose their position in

> ## "IT IS NOT OUR DIFFERENCES THAT DIVIDE US. IT IS OUR INABILITY TO RECOGNIZE, ACCEPT, AND CELEBRATE THOSE DIFFERENCES."
>
> **AUDRE LORDE**
> **BLACK AUTHOR AND POET**

the world, and that angered them—so much that they tried to protect it by any means necessary.

Over time—and using different forms of violence—they accomplished their ultimate goal of establishing a system that gave white men all kinds of privileges. They also created the idea that these privileges were just part of the pecking order of life. They claimed that those with the most physical strength and economic power would wind up with the most control and privilege. Anyone trying to overcome their lack of privilege, or calling privilege out, was fighting the "natural" order of things. In fact, not so long ago, there were studies done to scientifically prove that white men were biologically the most powerful beings on earth. But the research was based on lies, invented purely to keep people of color in their place.

Thankfully, we have made strides as a society, but this history of white male dominance still lives on and negatively affects all of us, especially those who come from communities that have been oppressed and silenced.

So how can we push for more change? One way is making sure everyone's voice is heard. A good starting point for that is representation.

WHAT IS REPRESENTATION?

Representation is when a person or a group of people become visible in an area of society (government, careers, sports, etc.) where (mostly white) men are perceived as the norm. Take pop culture for instance. *Black Panther* is seen as an important step in representation for Black people because he's a popular comic book and film character who's

Black and who has an African accent. The late Chadwick Boseman's incredible performance in the lead role proved a lot of things to Hollywood insiders. Movies with Black actors can be blockbusters! Huge audiences will embrace Black superheroes and also identify with and care about them! Still, the best part of *Black Panther*'s massive success is that it gave a huge community of people representation in a field where they didn't feel they had any.

The problem is, these characters are few and far between. In American culture, most of our main characters in pretty much all forms of media are white males, and the idea that this is normal—that white males are the baseline for heroes—drives a lack of representation.

Here's how it goes: white people create white male leads in stories. They do this over and over, until it's established as the norm by white audiences.

Then a nonwhite person and/or a woman is cast as the lead in a movie. This isn't the norm, because the industry has established that white men are the status quo.

A lot of people, challenged by something that's not the norm, don't go see that movie because they believe it's not for them, or see it and are forced to grapple with some personal questions. They complain online.

YOUR FAVORITE THINGS

Get out a notebook and write a list of all your favorite media—the movies, TV, books, comics, whatever, that you love. Do they reflect our diverse world? Do the characters in them have different cultural experiences than you? Is it possible that even some of the stories and characters you like uphold privileged ideas, even if they do that without making it obvious? This exercise shines a light on an interesting fact: the things we innocently like don't always reflect how the world treats people who are different than us.

And then the people who always cast the white guys say, "See? People only want to see white male leads onscreen." And then they create more white male leads. Then the cycle continues, and it feeds our privilege: "Look at the numbers! This is just how people are!"

More and more, though, we're learning that's *not* how people are. *Black Panther* didn't make $1.3 billion worldwide because only Black people saw it. Viewers of all races, ethnicities, and backgrounds were interested in a story and a cast of characters that they'd never seen before. And with the success of that representation comes even more representation.

This isn't just about race—more and more these days, so many different voices are finally getting heard because audiences around the world are asking for them and demanding them. People want to see more female characters, Asian and Latinx characters, gay and bisexual characters, handicapped characters, trans and nonbinary characters. These people are here, they've been here, and their stories are just as powerful as (if not more than) the majority of white stories we have grown up seeing—why deny us all a chance to see their stories onscreen? Because a studio executive says, "People just want to see white men"?

If we never get a chance to see and have compassion and understanding for all of our lives and stories, how can any of us ever understand humanity? It's through representation, and finally hearing and seeing points of view of storytellers from all races, genders, sexualities, and nationalities, that we start to fully grasp both how different—and alike—we all are. This is how entertainment can also create empathy. This is why representation matters.

WHY "NOT SEEING" IS NOT HELPING

Privilege exists. It's present in pretty much every part of society, whether we acknowledge it or not. With representation, we can start fighting privilege by cultivating compassion for each other.

Problem is, some people don't want to do that. They feel like being told they're privileged is like saying that all the struggles and hardships they had to face along the way don't count, or count less. Sometimes, they feel like they're being portrayed as a "bad person" for something they had absolutely no control over. More often than not, they're a little freaked out by how deep the rabbit hole goes. As University of Central Florida associate professor Ann Gleig writes on the subject of white privilege, "While individual white people are not to blame for policies that began before they were born, we are still benefiting from them at the—often grave—expense of Black Americans."

When privileged people realize the world is tilted in their favor, they begin to realize how much it affects everything in their lives. And that can make them feel really guilty and defensive.

But, guys, there is *nothing worse* than a person who doesn't recognize their own privilege. Fighting tooth and nail to prove that privilege is a myth does nothing but make us look totally unable to empathize with those around us. More important, it shows off just how privileged we are, because as boys, we have the ability to deny the stories of others from a seat of so-called "normality"—even more so if you're white and straight, like me.

And not to be grim, but as my friend Zach Anner said in an episode of my show *Man Enough*, "Anyone can join the disability community at any time." But it shouldn't take an accident to wake us up to our privilege.

The defensiveness around confronting one's own privilege doesn't always come out as yelling, or fighting, or arguing. Often, privilege is established by creating even more absence—by *not seeing* the issue. You hear this a lot with white privilege—"I don't see color, people are just people to me." The same is true for male privilege—"I don't care about gender." "It doesn't matter if you're a boy or a girl or if you identify as something else; all that matters is how talented or kind or _____ you are."

This might *sound* like finding common ground between two groups of people by erasing privilege. But all it's really erasing is the cultural experiences and the hardships of differently privileged groups. You may not "care about gender," but girls and women have had to deal with having the rules and confines of what it means to be female in a "man's world" pushed onto them for their entire lives. You may claim you "do not see color," but in reality, we all do. And it's offensive to people of color to claim we don't see color because what we are really saying is that we don't see *them*.

Let me go a little deeper on my experience with white privilege (and remember, if you feel like this part of my personal life doesn't relate to you, that's totally okay. You may relate to it in other ways, or have even been on the other side of a similar story to the one I am about to share). When I was ten and moved from LA to Oregon, my parents sent me to a small elementary school in the middle of nowhere with one Black kid named Jamal. One day while we were playing football at recess, much to my surprise I witnessed the other kids called him the N-word instead of his name. I can still remember how it felt in my body the first time I heard it. Thinking about it now, it makes me sick. I might have not known *exactly* what it meant—the full, horrific, extensive history of the word and its association with hatred and violence—but I knew it was not something that should ever be said by a white person. I can't imagine the pressure and pain of being the only Black kid in a small country town and being called that word.

While he may have laughed it off and pretended like it was okay to avoid drawing more attention to himself, my heart breaks for him that no one who was there said anything in his defense. That I, as a white kid, allowed these other white kids to say it because I was too scared that they would make fun of me or physically hurt me as I was already being bullied by the same guys who were calling him that name. I wish I would have stepped up and confronted them and let Jamal know that I would stand up for him. That would have been the right thing for me to do.

Later, in junior high, there was one multiracial kid on my soccer team named Leo. He was one of my closest friends. I distinctly remember being fourteen or so and staying in a motel for one of our soccer tournaments. We would always do crazy stuff that would lead to us almost getting kicked out, but hey, boys will be boys, right? Ugh. No, we were just idiots.

One night I learned that the game we always played where we knocked on someone's door and then ran off was called "[N-word] knocking." Jake, one of the white kids on the team, said we should play it, and I remember feeling incredibly uncomfortable and awkward—but when I looked over to Leo, who is part Black, he said, "Let's do it," so we started playing. For some reason, in my mind, Leo being okay with it meant that as a white person I had permission to play it.

Today, I know it wasn't on him to say anything—it was on me. And at the same time, no one had taught me about privilege and that it was my responsibility to use that privilege to speak up and call out behavior like this. I also didn't think about how that made Leo feel—how he, like Jamal in fifth grade, would put on a smile and appear to play along with the white kids. I didn't see this for what it really was: survival instinct.

And while I didn't know it at the time, my white privilege affected me, too. When I lost a race to a Black athlete, I would often make excuses because I was white and he was Black, which shows that I bought into the racist stereotype of Black people being naturally athletic and better at certain sports. And if someone was bothered by my excuses, I'd say something like, "My best friend is Black. I can say that." This is blatant white privilege.

However, it was what *didn't* happen to me that was most telling about my place of white privilege. The day I got my driver's license, I drove recklessly all over town. I broke every traffic law. I even bumped up against my buddy's car at a red light—for fun! An undercover cop followed me all the way to my friend's house, which happened to be in an all-white, upscale neighborhood.

At no point did this really scare me or make me fear for my life. That wasn't part of my upbringing. My parents never had to talk with me about what to do if I got pulled over. I never saw my parents mistreated by the police—getting a ticket for something they did wrong would have been the worst thing that could've happened to them, and oftentimes my dad was able to get out of tickets with his charm. In fact, if my parents ever didn't get out of a ticket, they would get upset: "But I was only going five miles over the speed limit, officer! Come on!" The privilege of simply being able to be upset because you WEREN'T able to talk your way out of a ticket, that lack of fear that you might be harmed because of your race, is white privilege in a nutshell.

Just because I didn't see it doesn't mean it wasn't there.

EXCUSES, EXCUSES

Okay, back to male privilege. There are all sorts of sayings that signal men can't—or won't—acknowledge their privilege. A famous one on the internet is #NotAllMen, a response used when women call out men for harmful behavior.

THE LEVEL PLAYING FIELD

The level playing field isn't a myth from folklore or pop culture, but it's an oral tradition that's been passed down from generation to generation. This story is based on the idea that everyone is born on the same level and whatever we accomplish in life is due to hard work, nothing more. But the truth is, history has proved that many groups of people have been systematically shortchanged by an unfair system built by people who hoard all the resources and power. The myth of the level playing field is mainly just an excuse to keep the unfair system intact.

The basic argument is that only some boys behave inappropriately toward people, but *not all* of them. And if that's true, then that means the whole argument against male behavior is invalid.

Another popular response to privilege is, "It's not my problem." If an issue doesn't matter to us or impact our lives, then fighting for it is a waste of time, so why bother, right? There's even "Men like that are terrible." This one may seem like a good way to confront privilege, but it's not—by saying "men like that" are terrible, it immediately casts the speaker as the "good guy."

If we don't stop making excuses and start accepting that as males we have privilege, there will never be a culture where everyone has the same opportunities and freedom to safely live out the lives they deserve.

A big part of dealing with male privilege is looking in the mirror and recognizing that whether we mean to or not, we benefit from how society has been built—some of us more than others, as I've mentioned.

If you're male, it's assumed that you're stronger, smarter, and more confident than everyone else (all the things we've covered in this book). You've been told it's YOUR world. If your bodily functions are treated as gross, it's funny gross, not cringe-and-gag gross. No one ever tells you that you'd be so pretty if you just wore makeup, or smiled more, or dressed in different colors.

And if you're white, you have probably never had to deal with the various levels of racism that have become a part of Black, Indigenous, and People of Color's (BIPOC) everyday lives. When you buy "flesh-colored" Band-Aids, they're in your skin tone. If you say something smart, no one's ever surprised about how well-spoken you are. When you go to the movies, or turn on the TV, or open a magazine you generally see people who look like you. No one tells you that you aren't welcome or you don't belong or to "go back to your own country."

If you're able-bodied, you've probably never thought twice about taking the stairs, or walking home, or running around a playground. You may even take things like catching a ball or typing on a computer for granted. When was the last time you were grateful for just being able to see or hear? It's often not until we lose something that we gain appreciation for the thing we had.

If you're straight, you've probably only worried about a girl turning you down or not liking you. You've never worried about getting beaten up just for being attracted to someone. You never hear a homophobic slur and feel anxiety and think, *That's me they're talking about.*

If you're Christian, you may spend all winter hearing and playing Christmas music, and it's pretty normal that most stores shut down on your holidays. But people don't act like you might blow up a building at any moment just because of the cross hanging around your neck or the Christmas tree in your window. Chances are your church has probably never been vandalized by members of other religions either.

Again: if you have more than one type of privilege, this isn't me calling you out or telling you that you're the problem. All you did was be born, just like the rest of us. But by benefiting from these privileges without seeing them, we're unable to help make things better, bit by bit. So let's acknowledge them, understand them, and then do our part to make this world kinder and safer for everyone.

Which leads to maybe the hardest part of dealing with privilege as a man.

We have to be brave enough to stand up to other guys and call them in . . . in the exact way that I DIDN'T when those boys called Jamal a racial slur.

I know—this can feel very difficult (and for boys who aren't white, you might feel unsafe doing this, which is completely understandable). As we talked about in the previous chapter, telling other guys to behave better violates the rules of the boys' club. These other guys might make you out to be a buzzkill, because they're just trying to have fun and you've brought up something complicated and uncomfortable. We all want to be liked, and by admitting that other guys aren't being fair—that the game is tipped in their favor, so being fair isn't an option they ever thought they should choose—it immediately makes us seem *difficult*. And being labeled as difficult can make us feel like an outcast.

But that's exactly why we have to do it. Privilege is only a problem when we don't acknowledge it and it becomes The Way Things Are. That makes it harder for women and those who don't identify as white, straight, cisgendered, able-bodied, etc., because people with privilege act like everyone is making a big deal out of nothing. But if we call out privileged language and behavior every day, we can start removing it from our lives. Every little bit of practice counts.

You might have heard of a football player named Colin Kaepernick, who has become a polarizing figure in the current political climate. People tend to either love him or hate him depending on which news station they watch or which way they vote. But should Colin's actions really be reduced to something being used to divide us? I personally don't think so.

Anyway, Colin was a player for the San Francisco 49ers who in 2016 started taking a knee during the national anthem before games in the wake of several Black people being killed by police. His goal was to bring awareness to and start conversations about racism in America. With the massive platform of the NFL, he could bring this message into homes across the country.

Some people knew it was a powerful, peaceful way to give voice to injustice. Other people were angry. "How dare this guy dishonor our flag and our anthem?" said some. "He's being paid a lot to play a game, not to lecture the world on race politics!" said others. But the most common angry response—among white people, mostly—was, "We

"WE MUST BRING OURSELVES TO REALIZE THAT [WE] ALL EMBODY **DIVINE POSSIBILITIES.** IF YOU GO INTO A GARDEN AND FIND ALL THE FLOWERS **ALIKE** IN FORM, SPECIES AND COLOR, THE EFFECT IS **WEARISOME** TO THE EYE. THE GARDEN IS **MORE BEAUTIFUL** WHEN THE FLOWERS ARE **MANY-COLORED** AND **DIFFERENT.**"

'ABDU'L-BAHÁ

FROM THE WRITINGS OF THE BAHÁ'Í FAITH

just wanted to watch a football game! Why do we have to turn a fun Sunday football game into this heavy conversation about race?" Well, if that's not an example of privilege, I don't know what is!

But Colin blocked out all of that noise. He continued to speak out even when other teams wouldn't hire him once he left the 49ers. He knew that his message was important, and he didn't let some code with other players, coaches, or even the NFL silence him.

All of us, no matter what our backgrounds are or how we identify, can take a page out of Colin's playbook. Confronting privilege in our daily lives can be hard, especially at first. But the more we do it, the less of a jarring, unpleasant thing it becomes. And once we're no longer afraid to face privilege head-on, we can begin to dismantle it.

ROOT SYSTEMS

Okay, so as boys, we've acknowledged that we've been benefiting from at least one form of privilege since we were born. Great—so now that we know, things will get better, right?

Not quite. The reason we aren't usually aware of privilege

in the wild is because the systems that support privilege run deep. Sometimes they show up in the form of big cultural institutions—education, policing, medicine—those parts of society that seem so big and important that we don't know where they begin or end. But other times, they're small comments or actions, the microaggressions, you don't even think of as mean.

The little things are often the worst—when privilege is exerted in a way that almost makes it seem so normal it can be blown off. These are what's known as "microaggressions," bigotries so small that often people don't even know they're performing them. For men, this can be anything from dismissing a TV show as "girl stuff" to telling another guy he "throws like a girl." They can even be set up as compliments—like telling a Black person they are "eloquent" or "well-spoken." I mean, why point this out—unless what the person is really saying is that Black people usually aren't.

Microaggressions can be hard to spot because the person is basically insulting someone or something in such a small way that it can be dismissed later: "You took what I said the wrong way. You're making a big deal out of this. That wasn't my intention." (This one is used all the time!) Except when you've experienced microaggressions every day for your whole life, you either learn to internalize them or recognize

INTENTION VS. IMPACT

Let's say I just spilled my drink on you and your new shirt. I felt bad and said "I'm sorry" because it was an accident. Even though it wasn't my intention, my actions had an impact on you: I ruined your new shirt. But you accept my apology because accidents can happen, and hey, I offer to get you a new shirt, so it's all good. Now, let's say I make a joke about one of your friends or say something to hurt your feelings. The impact of my actions is now emotional, and no matter what my intent was, it doesn't matter when compared to the harm that was caused. Making excuses like, "Don't be sensitive. I didn't mean it like that" just adds to the harm because responsibility isn't being taken. So regardless of our intentions, it's always more important to look at the impact of our actions. When we hide behind our intentions, it leaves the people we hurt still feeling hurt. But admitting you hurt someone even though you didn't mean to is one of the bravest—and most healing—things you could ever do.

them. And thankfully, more and more people are speaking out against this sort of behavior, especially when it comes to race.

On a slightly different note, have you ever heard the term "manspreading"? Me either until way too recently. Manspreading is basically when a guy sits down next to someone else with his knees really far apart, taking up more room than he actually needs. When he does this, he takes space from other people, and then the people next to him (especially in public places like a bus or subway) have to squeeze their legs tightly together or lean away from him. The thing is that most of the time, men like myself are not even aware we do it because we have been socialized to think that taking up space is what we are supposed to do. The problem is that while we think it's a natural way to sit and do so unconsciously, it's actually really rude and insensitive as we are taking away space from others. But because we are the ones doing it, unless someone says something, we never notice it.

Another example of a microaggression that oftentimes goes unnoticed (by men) and therefore rarely corrected is speaking over women (and other groups) and interrupting them during conversations. A study at George Washington University found that men interrupt 33 percent more often when speaking to women than they do when talking to other men. Men interrupted women 2.1 times per three-minute conversation, as opposed to the 1.8 times they interrupted other men. A similar study from Northwestern Pritzker School of Law showed that men even interrupt women more in the Supreme Court!

Of course, many guys don't *mean* to do this—we've just been trained to, because we're socialized to think that our voices matter more, that we deserve all that space on the subway because we're men (and, according to "men's rights group" Canadian Association for Equality, because it's cruel to crush our penises . . .). But once you start to notice these things, you'll see that everywhere you look, other men and boys—and even yourself—are doing it constantly. We're so worried about being man enough that we feel the need to make sure everyone sees us, feels us, and knows we're sitting/standing/walking there. It's almost like our presence must be known and seen for our value to matter.

But microaggressions are only half of the picture. On the other side of the spectrum are huge, hurtful attempts to instill in us an alternate version of history that glosses over America's troubled past. From a white privilege perspective, Columbus Day is a good example.

Columbus Day is supposedly a day to commemorate when Christopher Columbus "discovered" America on October 12, 1492. The holiday is often observed with depictions of Christopher Columbus as a brilliant Italian explorer, posing with his globe and scepter as he brings civilization to a lawless land. Except this didn't really happen—Columbus was actually looking for a passage to the Indies when he reached the Caribbean, as well as South and Central America. More so, many accounts leave out that when he arrived, he personally ordered the enslavement and obliteration of Native tribes.

Columbus's recasting as a noble explorer mostly came during the mass immigration of Italians to the United States in the late 1800s and early 1900s. Italian Americans saw him as a way to connect with the history of their new homeland. Over time, as Italians became more integrated into American society and viewed as white-adjacent, this idea was embedded further into our culture. Then Columbus Day emerged. It was a day we got off school, a day we celebrated the founding of America. . . .

Until recently, I've never had to think about Columbus the Monster, because I was taught that he was someone he really wasn't. I was taught he was a reason I should be proud to be Italian. In reality, his legacy is rooted in violence and conquest, and propping up Columbus has come at a huge cost to generations of Native Americans.

The good news is that people started having conversations about the truth of Columbus and calling out the

MINDFULNESS AND PRIVILEGE

Being aware of how we're privileged is something we should do every day. Like the other lessons in this book, checking one's privilege isn't something we do once—it's an ongoing, developing skill, and it's fundamentally about empathy and compassion. But we have to train our brains to stop and see how much of the world is designed to benefit us. For instance, the next time you are walking up a flight of stairs, think about how you would get around if you couldn't walk. Is the building you are in wheelchair accessible? If not, you wouldn't be able to reach the next floor. This bit of awareness allows you to recognize your able-bodied privilege. Try this act of mindfulness every day and keep track of your thoughts in a journal or meditate on it. Either way, the more you work on checking and being aware of your privilege, the more you will start to use your privilege in a way that benefits everyone around you. And there is nothing more "manly" than that.

injustice of revisionist history. Those conversations got louder and louder, and they made a difference. Indigenous

Peoples' Day is now celebrated across the country as an alternative to Columbus Day, recognizing the cultures that were here from the beginning.

CHECK AND CHECK AGAIN

If this chapter has made you uneasy, it means you're breaking out of your comfort zone. As you get older, regardless of how much or how little priviledge you have, you're going to mess up and say or do privileged things, and people might call you out on it. But you get to choose how to respond! Will you put on your armor and not let any of that feedback in because you feel attacked? Or will you take a breath and instead of being defensive, hear what the person has to say, and think about it from their perspective? Regardless, the harder you work at learning to check your privilege and see issues from another person's point of view, the more things will change for the better. Remember what we discussed in the smarts chapter: the best way to grow is admitting you need to.

And that's the good news: things *are* changing. They're just changing slowly, but now that privilege is being acknowledged regularly in our society—now that we're

> ## "WHEN THE WHOLE WORLD IS SILENT, EVEN ONE VOICE BECOMES POWERFUL."
>
> ### ▶ MALALA YOUSAFZAI ◀

identifying it and noticing how our actions feed into it—the next generation can confront it earlier than I did (and man, I wish I'd had this book at your age and been forced to step outside of my comfort zone and confront it).

Here's the cool part: You're the next generation. You're the future. Every day that you check your privilege and embrace empathy, you're making the future a little better.

And if that feels like a big responsibility, well, it is. But you got this. We got this. The world can't change itself. In fact, it's been waiting for us all this time.

BREAKING IT DOWN

PRIVILEGE IS HAVING THE DECK STACKED IN YOUR FAVOR EVEN IF YOUR LIFE IS HARD.

Privilege is being allowed to do or not do certain things because you are part of a privileged group.

PRIVILEGE IS REAL AND CAN BE HARD TO NOTICE.

Often, we are privileged in ways we don't see, ways that exist in an absence of certain experiences. Just because you can't see it doesn't mean privilege doesn't exist.

REPRESENTATION MATTERS.

All of our stories, no matter who we are or where we come from, deserve to be seen, heard, and felt. Representation matters because it helps reflect the diverse world we live in and builds empathy.

PRIVILEGE RUNS DEEP.

Privilege has been cemented into our society for centuries. By acknowledging it and calling it out for what it is in our daily lives, we can begin to take it apart, piece by piece.

6

BOYS WILL BE
MEN

HEADS UP! This chapter might make you, your parents, and your teachers uncomfortable, and that's okay. Before we dive in, though, take a breath and make sure you are ready to read about sex. Only you can know what you're ready for, and always remember you can skip parts of this chapter and come back to them later.

SEX: LET'S GET REAL

Here we are! The part of the book that might make you blush, cringe, or laugh from embarrassment. But before we go any further, let's try something. Count to seven. Seriously, stop reading and count to seven.

Done?

What did you think about?

Well, according to a widely accepted myth about boys, you just thought about sex.

After the publication of the Kinsey Report, the bible of sexual psychology studies, somehow the report's findings—that 54 percent of men think about sex several times a day—was twisted into this statistic that the average male thinks about sex every seven seconds. Somehow the misbelief that boys and men are thinking about sex nonstop and that we crave it and we're always supposed to be ready for it, became a common assumption.

But here's something you won't have to assume: this will be the most difficult part of the book. It highlights our insecurities and is full of very personal information. It's also got a lot of stuff that you might laugh at. We're going to talk about penises and pornography, a *lot*. (We're going to talk about harm and trauma, too.) The fact that it's so difficult to discuss—that we laugh at the very mention of sex and sexuality, because it's out-*raaageous* to even bring up—is the reason we have to talk about it. Because if we don't, it'll all remain taboo, a secret, or a joke. And when it's time to discuss it seriously, we won't know how. I sure didn't know how to. I mean, how can we understand something we can't even talk about?

Because we don't talk about it, we often get our information from less-than-ideal places. Boys learn a lot about sex from sources that either don't know what they're talking about (other boys, movies, music) or use unrealistic depictions of sex (pornography). And rarely, if ever, do we hear about how sex makes us feel emotionally, or what goes into having meaningful sex with a partner we care about.

This is because it's not only awkward for you to talk about sex, but it's also awkward for grown-ups to talk about it. Only recently have adults started to have access to more comprehensive resources to learn for themselves, let alone talk to kids about. When I was growing up, society referred to conversations about sex as "the birds and the bees," and it was seen as a conversation that happens one time and was always uncomfortable.

Sex is such a sensitive topic, and because so many people have a lot of insecurities and trauma around it, and not as much education or information, adults have a difficult time broaching the subject. But the more sex becomes an unspeakable taboo, the less boys and men actually learn about it in a positive and healthy way.

201

Ready for a little secret? Okay, here it is: sex . . . is a part of life. *Shhhhh*. Don't tell anyone. The last thing we would want is everyone talking about sex! That would be awful. I mean, it's not like it's the way that the majority of animals and human beings on this planet procreate, right?

So then why are we so embarrassed about it?!

I think it's because most of us learned that sex is something we should feel embarrassed or shameful about. Something we have to hide that we are interested in, like there's something wrong with the fact that our bodies are changing and we're having these new sexual feelings. How messed up is that?! It's part of being human, people!

Before we go any further: take a second right now and check in with how you're feeling. Do you feel excited? Nervous? Is your heart beating a little faster than it was in the last chapter? Have you shifted your body a little to make sure no one can read any of the bigger words on the page? Words like SEX? (Sorry, that was mean of me to make SEX so big on the page, but I couldn't resist. SEX. SEX. SEX. SEX. SEX. SEX. SEX. SEX. SEX. SEX. SEX. SEX. Okay, I'll stop now.)

Sometimes, it feels like there's no good time to really learn about sex, because everyone acts as though boys just somehow know everything about it from the moment we hit puberty. Like we are sexual beings with this innate knowledge and we have zero insecurities or questions. As we said in the chapter on being smart, there's this idea that boys should automatically know everything about everything, and nowhere is that truer than the conversation around sex, where admitting you don't know something reveals your inexperience to everyone you know. This leaves a lot of young men unable to just say, "I'm not ready for this." Or "Is this okay?" So we turn sex into a contest, or a dirty story, or a joke—anything to feel like we are cool, calm, and in control. When most of the time we aren't.

It's easy to laugh at sex, because society has taught us that it's funny, dirty, or inappropriate—and, if we're being honest, because laughter disguises our discomfort. To admit we don't know all about sex is the ultimate admission of ignorance, the kind of thing that could get you made fun of and laughed out of the boys' club. But the truth is we laugh so other guys won't know we're insecure, worried, or curious.

My hope, and maybe even my challenge, for you is that we can talk about this stuff and not laugh—that you can read this chapter and hold space for all your different feelings around it and try not to laugh. If you do, it's okay. I get it. But I hope, in this chapter especially, that I can continue to feel like a trusted friend, someone you don't have to

SEX 101

You may have learned about sex from your parents. Or maybe you've taken sexual education at school. There's a chance you've heard about sex from a sibling or a friend or a movie. Or perhaps you don't know much about sex at all—or you THINK you know but really don't have a clue. Well, for the purposes of this book, "sex" is any physical act of pleasure (kissing, touching, intercourse, etc.) between two consenting partners of any gender.

anxiously giggle around, someone with whom you can talk about this as honestly as we have talked about body image and not feeling smart enough.

I've said it before, but it's worth saying again: I'm writing about sex from my experience as a heterosexual guy, so if some of the content here doesn't quite apply to you, feel free to just tune in to what does.

NUTS AND BOLT

At some point in every boy's life, we're told that our penis is doing our thinking for us. So in addition to the myth that we're thinking about sex every seven seconds, we're also supposedly walking around with this second brain below our belts that controls us. Apparently, as boys hit puberty, our penises become all-powerful to us.

But nobody talks about how sensitive they actually are.

Strictly physically, our penises and testicles (which produce testosterone) are incredibly sensitive, and a hit to them is a surefire way to take the biggest, strongest guy down. Did you know that there are four thousand nerve endings in our penises alone? But the same thing that makes them sensitive is also what makes sex pleasurable. In other words, our greatest weakness is also one of our biggest strengths. But it's not just the physical sensitivity of the penis that causes issues.

Too often, it feels like the whole world is staring at our penises, waiting for them to be used in one way or the other. As guys, the way the world sees our penises can quickly become the way we see ourselves. Our penises become us, and the world views us through them. But just like our penises, us boys are sensitive. That doesn't mean we're weak—in fact, our sensitivity is what gives us pleasure in life.

I remember the first time that I ever felt like my penis was inadequate. I was eleven years old, and one of my friends—Jason, I'll call him—was a year older than me, and more physically developed than I was, and he told me that he had pubic hair and asked if I had any. I didn't. He pulled down his shorts and showed me his penis. Even though by this age I had already seen pornographic images of men's penises, I immediately noticed the differences between my penis and Jason's.

Mine hadn't really developed yet, and I had never seen someone's penis who I knew. Everything seems to register differently when it's your friend, especially in terms of comparison and competition. This was another kid, just like me, and yet his penis more closely resembled the images I had seen in magazines and on the internet than mine did. It was bigger and hairier, and it made me and my prepuberty kid penis feel like I was somehow lacking, abnormal, immature. Like I was less of a boy and would always be less of a man.

Of course, this wasn't the case. Jason just hit puberty before me. The only real cure to my feelings of being less than was the last thing I had at the age of eleven: patience. My penis would eventually grow with me; life would go on and I'd learn that there's so much more to me than one body part, but try telling that to eleven-year-old me.

See, because no one ever sat me down and talked to me about the fact that my penis would soon start to grow, and get hair, and start to have erections and that all penises look different, I was caught blindsided and I couldn't help but wonder what was wrong with me. I felt pressured—as though the world was going to find out that Jason had a bigger penis and that I hadn't hit puberty yet. What's especially painful about the story (in retrospect, of course) is that the mature thing to do would've been to admit I wasn't physically or emotionally ready to worry about this—that my body, and my mind, were literally *not there yet.*

But that's tough, especially with our penises. We're told they're important, that they make us a man. That they should be perfect—*now.* But perfect is a myth. Part of respecting your body as a man is respecting its development. And instead of listening to everyone else's opinions on our penises, we should acknowledge their sensitivity and let them grow, change, and work on their own time. Because they are OUR penises, not anyone else's.

NO SEX? NO PROBLEM.

This might be a record-scratch moment. No sex? NONE? Well, we can't have an honest sex talk without talking about *not having sex*, and this seems like as good a time as any to do it.

I think it's totally okay if someone makes the personal choice to be chaste or abstain from sex until marriage. It might seem like an old-fashioned idea, but we shouldn't judge someone for wanting to stay a virgin, just like we shouldn't judge someone for their sexual orientation or other parts of their experience. If living sex-free feels like the right decision for you, just know that despite what you might think, chastity isn't about repressing your sexual desires. In my view, chastity is more about learning to look at people holistically. That means seeing others beyond their physical appearance or sexuality and cherishing all of the qualities that make them human. Essentially, you're putting more of an emphasis on making contact with someone else's soul rather than contact with their body.

For some people, not wanting to have sex is just how they're wired. People who are asexual (or "ace") can experience little to no sexual attraction. So whatever the reason might be for waiting to have sex or not wanting to, just remember that we all deserve to be accepted for who we are.

HEADS UP! To any boy reading this who knows they're not straight, I want you to know: you're you, and you are awesome. You're no more or less of a man than anyone else. Your heart and soul matter. Your spirit matters. You matter. Who you are, as you are, is enough.

"THAT'S SO GAY": SEXUAL ORIENTATION IN THE BOYS' CLUB

Earlier in the chapter on bravery, we talked about how "wimp" is shorthand for weak, or not cool, or girly. But in my high school, when one dude was calling out another for being cowardly or weak, "wimp" wasn't the term I heard the most. It was definitely "gay."

Being called "gay" wasn't just being labeled soft or not manly; it was being called different. It was almost like if you were called "gay," it was worse than being called a girl because you were seen as some sort of traitor to your own gender. You weren't someone people wanted to hang out with, lest they get labeled "gay," too, just for being friends with you. Of course, if you got upset or defensively fought against it, that just made you seem all the gayer for showing emotions, because as we already learned, we aren't supposed to show emotions. If someone found a way to work the word "gay" into your nickname, forget it; your reputation was over.

For the record, I went to high school a while ago, when homophobia was still broadly tolerated, and when there were way fewer "out" celebrities than there are now. There was no Jim Parsons or Lil Nas X when I was a kid. But just because there are more gay celebrities who have representation in the magazines, on TV, and in movies, it doesn't mean the struggle is over. According to a Youth Risk Behavior survey from as recently as 2019, 10 percent of LGBTQ (lesbian, gay, bisexual, trans, and queer or questioning) students were threatened or injured with a weapon on school property, 34 percent were bullied on school property, and 28 percent were bullied electronically.

This also translates to some of the other issues we've discussed in previous chapters. Plenty of guys get scared of coming off as gay because of the fear that it could hurt their social standing, so they avoid any instance of intimacy, including physical contact or eye contact, with other boys. Even body image issues relate to it—on an episode of my show *Man Enough*, actor Javier Muñoz, who is gay, told me how he felt the need to be physically big in order to stay safe in a world where he might get assaulted.

"In the eighties and nineties, growing up in New York City, if I was by myself and in certain contexts where maybe I wasn't welcome, my survival instinct clocks the situation and says, *Am I small enough that these guys feel they can start something with me, that they can take me?*" he told me. "Or *Am I so big and aggressive that they are going to have to think twice?*"

All of this makes me wonder: Why is someone's queerness such a threat, especially to straight guys?

Well, if what we've learned so far is that the boys' club rules specifically tell you not to display emotions around guys, then being gay seems like the ultimate violation of that, right?

But if we're being honest, homophobia is learned. According to psychology professor Gregory M. Herek, straight people with negative attitudes toward people who are gay are notable for not having much, or any, actual contact with the queer community and have limited societal values. That seems to suggest that what they think about gay people is based on what they've heard from the media, religious organizations, and the people around them—especially other straight guys.

The problem with that is there's no empathy. If you're queer or trans, nothing gets solved when a straight person tells you that you're wrong, or that you're confused, or that some people don't believe that you exist. Then on top of that, in certain circles your safety is often in question in a real and scary way.

> ## "I THINK I'VE SHOWN THE WORLD I'M A **FIERCE** COMPETITOR. BUT I'VE ALSO SHOWN THEM THAT I AM A FIERCE **HUMAN BEING**."
>
> ### ▶ ADAM RIPPON ◀
>
> **OLYMPIC FIGURE SKATING CHAMPION AND GAY ACTIVIST**

Homophobia also puts a stigma on male intimacy that's unfair and creates constant fear. Suddenly, straight guys aren't allowed to hug, cry, or even say something nice to one another, or if they do, they have to preface it with something like "no homo." That's a huge plate of very weak armor standing between us and our fellow boys. Let's take it off and leave it by the side of the road. Let's listen to one another and remember the idea of compassion over comprehension. You don't have to understand someone's experience to accept them, support them, and want them to be happy.

READY OR NOT, HERE I . . .

One summer day, my friend Jason (with the fully grown penis) and I went to the local lake for the afternoon with his older brother and their friends. The lake had two-seater paddleboats that you could rent, and he and I took one out. The plan was to go out in the paddleboat, bring his back-pack, and, once we were out in the middle of the water, pull out his dad's porn magazines and look at them with no one else around.

Instead, when we reached the center of the lake, Jason pulled out one of the magazines, opened it, and started touching himself. I didn't know what to do. I felt paralyzed as this was the first time I had ever seen another boy's erect penis and the first time I had seen anyone masturbate. I had no idea what was happening and had never masturbated before either. So I did what I had been trained to do as a boy.

Fake it.

While trying to not look uncomfortable, I turned my back to him and pretended to do the same. Then a few minutes later he said he had "finished." I didn't know what that meant, and after a few frustrating, confused moments, I told him I needed to pee, so we went back to shore.

On what could have been a perfect summer day I felt ashamed and insecure. My penis couldn't do what his did, it didn't look like his did, and therefore it wasn't good enough. And in my mind, it never would be. Was there something wrong with me? Would my body ever be able to do what his did? Was I going to be "behind" forever?

It's tough for me to tell that story because honestly it has haunted me for a long time, but it's important that I do. Hopefully I can help boys avoid putting each other in sexual situations they're not prepared for. And maybe I can help boys who've been in them feel less alone.

Because boys are told that we are supposed to think with our penises, our penises are supposed to know everything. We're supposed to follow our penises like they're metal detectors and brag about them like they are something we had any control or say in developing. Like we chose our penises and they are our prized possession. This is so ridiculous.

But for young boys just learning about their sexuality and their bodies, trying to push sex and sexual situations on us, to make us think we should somehow be sexually curious or active before we're ready is harmful. These are the roots of boys' sexuality, and if boys feel like they *have* to be sexual as soon as possible, they could base their sexuality on false information and feelings of obligation.

You should never feel like you *have* to have any part of sex. You should never be put in a situation you aren't ready for sexually, physically, or emotionally. Your brain is still developing, and every experience you find yourself in sexually, especially during the time when your body is changing, has a massive effect on the way you will see yourself sexually for years to come. This isn't to say that sexual curiosity and things like masturbation are unhealthy. In fact, our sexual impulses are completely normal and natural, just like our instinct to eat when we are hungry. But when our bodies are changing and our hormones are raging, it can feel like sex is

"IF MEN WERE SOCIALIZED TO **DESIRE LOVE** AS MUCH AS THEY ARE TAUGHT TO **DESIRE SEX**, WE WOULD SEE A CULTURAL **REVOLUTION**. AS IT STANDS, MOST MEN TEND TO BE **MORE CONCERNED** ABOUT SEXUAL PERFORMANCE AND SEXUAL SATISFACTION THAN WHETHER THEY ARE CAPABLE OF **GIVING** AND **RECEIVING LOVE**."

BELL HOOKS

the only thing that matters (here's another secret: it isn't!).

Because sex is all around us, all the time (in movies, TV, music, etc.) yet nobody seems to want to talk about it openly and honestly, it's easy to feel confused and desperate to understand what sex is really about. In a search for answers, boys often turn to pornography, which is what we're going to unpack next.

HARDCORE

Given how much porn is on the internet, and how fast our phones are these days, it's almost inevitable that people are going to experience porn at a very young age. And for young men, who are constantly told that they're just penises on two legs, the pressure to learn about sex from porn is overwhelming, especially when no one is talking about it ("it" being both sex and porn).

There's a lot of debate about whether porn is morally right or wrong. I'm not going to tell you one way or another, because maybe you are curious about sex and have watched porn a few times. I don't want you to feel shame. But more important, I think labeling something bad or dangerous immediately makes you want to try it more.

When I was a kid, I always wanted to push boundaries (I still do). If someone told me something was bad or off-limits, I wanted to know why, and it just made me more curious to experience whatever it was. Was that rapper making music that made people mad? I had to listen to his music. Was that movie going to scare the crap out of me and give me nightmares? We had to watch it! (Just before bed.)

That said, there are some things about porn that aren't acknowledged enough. First, and most important, mainstream porn isn't the best place to learn about sex because it's an inaccurate representation of what sex can be, especially to someone who's just learning about it. Sex involves a lot of trust and communication to be truly enjoyed, and two people with idealized bodies slamming into each other while screaming swear words is *NOT* what sex is or looks like to most people. Learning about sex from porn is like learning to fish by watching a guy blow up sharks with dynamite. There's like one guy in the world who can do it that way, and everyone else would just end up blowing themselves up. It's not at all realistic.

But for many kids, it feels like porn is the only way to find out about sex. For me—and a lot of guys, straight or queer—porn was our only "sex education." There was literally nowhere else to turn that felt safe to ask questions. And often it wasn't even about fantasies; it was about trying to understand what sex looked like and how to have it because the last thing any boy wants is to not know how to do something. Unfortunately, young people wanting to know about sex makes a lot of grown-ups uncomfortable because they worry they might say the wrong thing. Because remember, most of the time adults don't know what to say because they didn't have a healthy sex education either. So in some ways, we are all learning together.

Too often these awkward conversations with grown-ups only scratch the surface and mostly involve "When two people love each other very much" kind of talk. Which doesn't help a teenage boy who, say, wants to know how to talk to his partner about consent and pleasure, or who's worried about being able to put a condom on. Porn does the opposite—it starts the student on "advanced mode" the minute they start the game. What most of us really want to know is something in-between, but we also want people to be super honest with us and stop treating us like little kids. So when the options for learning about sex are your parents, a teacher, some guidance counselor, or the ultra-intense-but-not-realistic world of porn, a lot of boys pick porn.

Okay, second: porn may physically depict people having sex, but it's an act. It's theater. The people in porn are performers. They are getting paid and they are having sex in a way that's often meant to be extreme, or play to a camera. They are cast as actors by porn companies based on the way their bodies look. Also, most porn actors have had surgeries or taken steps to enhance parts of their body, including their boobs, penises, and vulvas. So when we watch porn, we start to believe that's how sex is supposed to be, or *has* to be. And when we look in the mirror and don't see the bodies that we see in porn, or we engage in sexual exploration that looks and feels nothing like porn appears to look and feel, it leaves us making unfair comparisons and feeling bad about ourselves.

This raises the question: Why are we so focused on these idealized bodies? Why do we want to see fantasy people have sex? And the answer is, because sex is complicated, and watching other people have it activates parts of our brains that excite us and keep us wanting more. After all, sex is why you and I are here in the first place. Seeing other peope have sex can turn us on, and it makes us ask questions about ourselves. It makes us think and look in the mirror. Porn offers an escape, and instead of making us think about our comfort zones or our regard for the human body, it gives us an idealized version of things. Seemingly with no strings attached. (But keep reading. . . .)

Third: as I mentioned, porn is an industry. It's a business, and businesses are about making money. That's why there's so much porn out there—because they know that people who like it will pay top dollar for it. And because porn is an industry, the people who make it want us to watch it *constantly*. In the same way that alcohol companies don't *really* care how responsibly we drink and vaping companies don't *really* care how much we smoke, most of the companies making porn don't *really* care about how educated we are in the ways of sex, safety, sexuality, and emotion. In fact, the less educated we are and the younger we are, the better, because that's when our minds are the most impressionable. If they can get us interested young, they know they have a good chance of having customers for life. At the end of the day, our clicks and money are what's at stake here for them.

Fourth: with its wide variety, high speed, and easy accessibility, porn can get us hooked on instantaneous pleasure. And the way it does this is through a fascinating chemical in our brain called dopamine.

DOPAMINE: HOW IT WORKS

Dopamine was first synthesized in London in 1910 by George Barger and James Ewens. Later, in Sweden, Arvid

Carlsson and Nils-Åke Hillarp figured out its role as a neurotransmitter, a chemical in your brain. These scientists' work is very involved and dry, and if I'm being real with you, I don't fully understand all the data (admitting we don't know is how we grow, right?). But I've managed to understand the basics of their discovery and I'll do my best to explain it to you!

Essentially, our brains are like supercomputers that are constantly processing information at light speed. Each of our brains has this thing called a "reward center," which is a complex system that releases chemicals that make us feel good or bad depending on what we are experiencing. Dopamine gives us a quick, natural high that makes us want to repeat whatever it is we're doing. The real reason we have this is to help us survive and make positive choices, ideally so that the human race can thrive.

To paraphrase *Neuroscience News*, the relationship between dopamine and our neuropathways is kind of like a hiking trail in the woods. Before your brain rewards you for something, there is no trail, so you can't hike. But once you give your brain a taste of something it likes, it rewards you with dopamine, which makes you want to experience that thing again. So dopamine is kind of like your brain using a machete to chop through the bush so you can experience more of the good things it likes.

Social media is another thing that taps into that same reward center. The first time we post a video or photo, we do it just for fun. But then someone likes it or leaves a comment, which makes us feel good, right? And because it feels good, our brains produce more dopamine, and the rest of our body wants more of it, so we post again and again. Before we know it, we can become dependent on posting on social media because it makes us feel popular and admired. That's also why if one of our posts doesn't get many likes, we can start to feel bad about ourselves. Our brains were expecting a hit of dopamine, and it didn't come.

But scientists have found that not all dopamine hits are the same in the reward center of our brain, and some rewards are bigger than others. And can you guess what gives our brains one of the biggest dopamine hits?

SEX.

The way I understand it, sex isn't like using a machete to clear a trail; sex is like driving a gigantic bulldozer through the jungle and flattening everything in its path. It's the big, sweet, intoxicating dopamine hit that our minds and bodies crave. The dopamine hit from sex is our brains saying, "Great, that felt amazing. Let's do it again!"

But in the world of on-demand instant gratification that the internet has created, we want that dopamine hit *now*.

And masturbating to porn is a really easy and dependable way to get it. But soon we want more—we want the high to feel bigger, stronger. So we watch more porn, masturbate more often, and soon, oftentimes without even realizing it, our brains develop a dependency on it.

There's also one more way that porn companies create dependency, and that's through the use of something called "random reward theory." Which is the same thing that social media apps use to keep us mindlessly scrolling on the app for hours and hours.

Have you ever been in a public place, like a restaurant, looked around, and noticed that EVERYONE is on their phones, just swiping away? Well, the reason is because apps and social media have been scientifically designed to retain the user's attention via complex algorithms based in random reward theory. Basically, what this means is that scientists figured out that by not putting an end to the feed on your social media app, and by creating an algorithm that shows you images and videos that are based on your preferences, it can predict what you will like and make sure it gives it to you.

So while you are scrolling, your brain goes into a state of anticipation hoping for either a win or a picture or video that will excite it. Your brain is literally scrolling for a dopamine hit, and when it doesn't get it, it keeps scrolling. Then

GUT CHECK

EXERCISE YOUR BRAIN

The reward center in your brain loves those dopamine spikes, so giving your brain a break from social media and video games is a great way to supply it with the healthy fuel it needs. Try this: When you feel an urge to pick up a phone or tablet, go on social media, or play a video game, see if you can slow down your brain by taking a few deep breaths. What are you feeling in your body? Do you feel anxious? Are you distracting yourself from doing something you need to do, or uncomfortable emotions? This week, try to pay attention and instead energize your brain with an activity that is a bit heathier. Go for a walk, read a book (not on a tablet), do a puzzle, work out, basically try to do anything besides chasing that dopamine hit you are craving. After, see if you notice anything different about how you feel. Do you have more energy? Are you more alert? Do you feel happier?

when it gets it, it feels good and wants a bigger or better one, so it tells you to keep scrolling. That's why social media feeds show you photos similar to ones you have already liked and send you notifications when someone likes your post or leaves a comment. Everything is programmed so that you'll want to stay glued to your phone, and it works by manipulating the dopamine in your brain! Unbelievable, right?

I'm not just telling you all this because I've read a lot of studies about this topic—I'm the effect in the flesh. I was introduced to porn when I was ten years old by two kids from a very religious family. It was innocent at first. It felt dangerous and like we were doing something we weren't supposed to, but also exciting. Their family had a computer with the internet (mine didn't yet. I know, I know; I'm old) and we would look at images of naked women whenever their parents fell asleep. Soon, my dopamine-hungry brain wanted more, but I didn't have any access to it.

Then when I met Jason and he introduced me to his dad's porn magazine collection, which was more graphic. I became fascinated. So after that day on the paddleboat, I taught myself how to masturbate, and started masturbating to porn whenever I could find it (which can become unhealthy, as you'll see).

By college, I would sometimes spend hours and hours in front of the computer looking at porn. Sometimes every day, sometimes multiple times a day. And sometimes I would even choose to not hang out with my friends or go to parties so I could look at it. Porn was a friend to me when I was depressed and a reward for me when I was happy. But no matter when or why I chose to use it, porn always left me feeling the same way about myself—ashamed.

Ironically, as soon as I felt that shame my brain told me I needed to watch more porn to make that shame go away. And guess what? Watching more just made me feel more ashamed!

Before I knew it, I was in this harmful cycle that gave me anxiety and made me depressed. This is what dependency is like—having a habit that feels almost impossible to break. And that feeling of shame never went away either.

Eventually, I used porn to numb myself and disconnect from emotions that made me uncomfortable and afraid. If I felt sad or lonely or scared, I could always go to porn to help me momentarily forget about what I was feeling. But it was only a temporary fix, and those feelings were always waiting for me, except now they felt even more overwhelming.

Honestly, as I write these very words, I can still feel a big wave of anxiety washing over my body, so I'm taking a deep breath and allowing myself to feel it. Memories are now popping up and I'm noticing there's still a part of my brain trying to convince me that the way to make the anxiety disappear is to stop writing this book and look at porn.

That's how powerful dopamine is, and why dependency on things like porn, alcohol, drugs, and, yes, even social media can have a negative impact on our lives. Dependency can desensitize us and distract us from the feelings and situations that make us feel, when the healthier (and braver) choice is to face those situations head-on, feel those feelings, and work through them. But it will take time, patience, strength, and bravery to finally let ourselves feel all the feelings we're running away from. What could be more manly than that?

THE PORN IN YOUR POCKET

Part of the problem with how sex reaches us today is that it's readily available through our phones. Not only do smartphones give us access to countless pornographic websites, but phone cameras allow us to take nude photos and send them to one another. Whether it's sexting—sending sexual messages or fantasies—or taking nude pictures, we not only have the ability to communicate sexually with someone at a moment's notice, but sometimes it feels like we are expected to and expect our crushes or partners to. And this, in turn, creates a lot of unhealthy behavior.

Because boys often want to seem like the alpha, or like they're "doing what everyone else is," they'll pressure partners to send them nudes and then show them to other boys to prove they can get someone to make porn just for them. This causes problems in a lot of ways: for instance, boys might pressure their friends or partners to send them pictures they might not be comfortable taking. If the person taking the picture is under a certain age, it's also illegal. And, if that nude picture gets out—if guys share it around, or post it online as a way to feel manly or maybe out of bitterness and rejection (we'll talk more about that in chapter seven)— it can ruin the lives of both the person in the picture and the people around them. And if you sneak a sexy picture of someone without them knowing? That is a betrayal of trust and it's also illegal.

There are countless stories of families having to leave town or, even worse, young people dying by suicide because a picture they sent to someone in confidence made the rounds in their community. These kids felt so embarrassed and humiliated that they thought there was no way out. This is bullying taken to the extreme and is one of the worst things you could ever do to someone. So while it might seem harmless to snicker with your friends about a nude pic someone sent you, it is never harmless.

WHAT IS...

CONSENT?

"Consent" is when someone gives permission and voluntarily agrees to the proposal or desires of another. This generally means the giving of permission to engage with another person, usually sexually or emotionally. Once someone has told you that they willingly want to do something with you, you have their *consent*. But consent can be changed or revoked at any time, meaning that someone can give consent and then suddenly feel uncomfortable and take it away. If this happens the partner must immediately acknowledge it and stop engaging.

It also is a huge violation of CONSENT. We'll break down what consent is in more detail shortly, but in this instance—if someone sends you an explicit picture, there's an understanding that they sent it to you and only you. To share it without their permission is taking away their right to privacy.

So is sending a dick pic without consent. It's a bummer that we even have to talk about this, but it's a thing:

guys (gay or straight) sending unsolicited pictures of their penises to people. Why would someone ever want to receive a picture of a person's penis without asking?! Believe it or not, researchers from Singles in America found that 80 percent of gay or bisexual men and 50 percent of women had received a dick pic—and that *90 percent of those people never asked for one!* Someone sent them a picture of their penis, totally unsolicited. *Why?*

Part of it definitely feels like porn—because there's access to so much of it, we see ourselves in it and think our penises matter enough that we should lead with that. But in many ways, it's equivalent to shoving one's penis into someone's face without asking. So, guys, please: unless we are 1,000 percent positive someone wants to see our penis (meaning they've given consent), do not send them a picture of it!

SEX IS CONSENSUAL AND CONNECTED

Most likely, you are a few years away from being ready to have sex. And that's okay. Sex isn't something that should be rushed. I was twenty the first time I had sex, and unfortunately it wasn't a good experience at all. Ask most people

HEADS UP! This section of the book could be painful for you to read, especially if you have had anyone violate your boundaries and touch you sexually or force themselves on you. If you are a victim of sexual assault or abuse, let me start by saying that I believe you and I am so sorry that happened to you. I can only imagine how confusing and painful it has been for you, and it is not your fault. Is there a grown-up, a teacher, a counselor, or maybe a friend's parent in your life who you trust and feel safe with? Is there a school staff member or coach who makes you feel like the important person you are? Well, if you haven't told anyone yet, these are the kind of people you can tell. And I hope you do. What happened to you doesn't define you. You are loved, you are seen, you are believed, and you are enough.

about their first time having sex, and if they're being honest, a lot of them will tell you something like, "Oh man, it was so weird" or "Well, I'm glad I got it over with. . . ." This is because we get all caught up in what sex is supposed to be from movies, TV, books, the people around us, and for many of us, from porn. But when we actually start having sex, we don't become some chiseled hunk undressing our partner.

The armor is off and it's just us, with all the feelings—and mishaps—that come with being human.

Here are some of the unexpected things that can happen to men during a sexual experience: premature ejaculation, where the man has an orgasm quicker than he would like; erectile dysfunction, where the man can't get an erection; or, most simply—and sometimes, most devastatingly—finding yourself actually not emotionally or spiritually ready to have sex and being worried that you're going to upset your partner by saying no or "Hey, I'm not feeling comfortable. I want to wait."

The thing is, at some point in every man's life, he will experience one or all of these things—they're perfectly normal and happen to millions of people every day because we are not robots, we are humans, and so much of sex is actually influenced and affected by our emotional state. What's problematic is the shame heaped upon us when they happen, and the pressure we put on ourselves to perform and to be ready for it and want it all the time. The people we see in the media and in porn don't have these problems— therefore, it must be our fault. (Actually, the actors in porn oftentimes take pills and get shots just to make sure those things don't happen on camera.) When these things happen to us, we can feel broken and like we're failures.

Anyway, back to my first time. I was dating a girl who really wanted to have sex before I felt comfortable. It wasn't a healthy relationship, and she pressured and eventually forced me to have sex with her before I felt ready. It's important to know that there is more than one way to make someone do what they want you to do. They can pressure you emotionally or physically (sometimes both), play mind games with you, and even be verbally abusive so that you bend to their will.

In my case, we'd had conversations about how I wanted to wait to have intercourse, and yet one time when we were consensually kissing and touching each other while naked, she made a move that transformed what we were doing into sexual intercourse even though she knew I wanted to wait—even though I hadn't given consent and said yes.

I was in shock and hurt and confused. I stopped what we were doing and asked her why she would do that. She told me that we had already been "so close" to having sex, and now that we had done it, what was the big deal? So, not only did she violate my trust, she then insinuated that my feelings and boundaries weren't important or valid.

When I tried to explain that (to me) what we had been doing wasn't sex, she told me I was wrong. She claimed it was all the same and that we had basically been having sex this whole time. She then said things like "If you really loved me, this wouldn't be a big deal," which made me feel like I was being unreasonable and mean. This is an example of gaslighting, the manipulation tactic we talked about earlier.

Somehow, after my boundaries and trust had been betrayed I was left feeling bad for feeling upset about it in the first place. Unfortunately, like many people who have experienced similar things, I cared more about keeping her happy than being true to myself and later ended up going along with her desires while abandoning myself and my own sense of boundaries.

To cope with the regret and harm that the first time caused, I started questioning my manhood. I was a healthy, fit twenty-year-old guy. *What's wrong with me? Am I not a man?* Now, looking back, what I've realized is that if there was anyone or anything to blame, it wasn't me. She crossed a big line that day, and what she did and said wasn't okay. Yet it felt like she, along with all the members of the boys' club, were in the background, telling me I needed to have sex even if I wasn't ready.

At the time, I wanted to stay true to my spiritual beliefs and wait to have intercourse with the one person I wanted to spend my life with. I had told her this, but it didn't matter to her, which felt awful because I wasn't being heard or honored. Then the fear, shame, and self-doubt poured in. Things were no longer black-and-white but shades of gray. I didn't know what to believe or even what I wanted anymore, and my memories of what happened morphed and changed to accommodate my reasons for staying in the relationship. I mean, we were already doing other sexual things. Maybe it was my fault because there was a part of me that was curious what intercourse would feel like and deep down I wanted it to happen? Every thought and feeling I had about it seemed to contradict the other.

What I am describing to you right now is just part of the confusion and emotional pain that can come with sexual assault. You might think just because you want to have sex that it means you are ready, but sex requires two people deciding that they are ready together and then checking in with each other throughout the experience in a process called "consent."

Consent is really simple:

IF IT'S NOT AN ENTHUSIASTIC YES, IT'S A NO.

And if you ignore the desires of the person you're being sexually intimate with, then that's sexual assault—even if they don't say the word no; and especially if they are drinking alcohol or using drugs. An enthusiastic yes must be given (and not just one time, but every time) for you to be sexually intimate with someone.

LET'S TALK ABOUT

FRENCH FRIES AND CONSENT

Imagine having lunch with someone you really like. You both agreed to go somewhere you can get french fries to share, and you get some super expensive rare flavor of fries (have you had truffle oil on your fries?!). You are so excited for them to try your favorite fries, but then as you hand them some, they decide they don't want them anymore. Man, that's a bummer. But does that mean you should talk them into eating them even after they changed their mind? If you really like this person, you wouldn't want to make them feel bad for it, right? They might have a bunch of reasons why they don't want the fries anymore. Maybe their stomach is upset, maybe the fries just don't sound as good as they did ten minutes ago. Maybe they aren't eating carbs today. Whatever the reason, you don't make them feel bad or guilty, you just say, "Okay, I get it. Want to get something else instead?"

Now what if they start eating the fries but after one or two decide they don't want any more? They feel bad saying it, but they changed their minds and are no longer in the mood for fries. Even though it might hurt your feelings because they're your favorite and you'd been looking forward to sharing them, and you had agreed to share, you say, "Okay, I understand. No worries at all. It happens." You do not try to force them continue to eat fries after they said they didn't want to. I mean, who wants fries shoved down their throat?

And what if you left the room to go ask for ketchup and your friend suddenly falls asleep? Well, when you come back you might wake them up, because taking a nap in a restaurant is kind of weird, but you definitely wouldn't try to make someone who is sleeping eat fries, just because you had previously agreed on sharing fries, right? Of course you wouldn't!

You get what I'm saying, right? Nobody wants to eat french fries after they say they don't want them. No matter what the situation is, or no matter how good they are, there is never a reason to make anyone eat fries with you if they don't want to. And by fries . . . yes, I mean SEX. Good chat.

Most instances of sexual assault are reported by women, but many boys and men experience it every day. Unfortunately, the rules of masculinity don't protect boys or give them permission to reveal what happened because boys are expected to be the pursuer of sex and always ready to have it.

When you get older, if you for even a second feel like you aren't ready to have sex or do something sexual even after you said you were, it's okay to say NO. It doesn't make you weak or less than. It doesn't mean you aren't a man. It makes you a human. And just like I didn't honor my feelings that day on the bridge and jumped because I felt the pressure of the boys waiting for me below, at twenty years old I ended up doing the same thing with sex.

The difference is it would have been like someone pushed me off the bridge instead of me jumping by myself. And instead of telling anyone about it, I kept it to myself because the rules of masculinity made it clear that having sex made me a man, and not wanting it made me weird. But listen to me when I say this: there's nothing manly about doing something you don't want to do, especially when it's as emotional, confusing, and complicated as sex. The manliest thing we could ever do is honor our emotions and listen to our bodies even if it makes it awkward or uncomfortable for someone else.

Vulnerability, trust, and communication are the most important building blocks for safety, and safety is a vital part of any kind of intimacy, sexual intimacy included. If we're comfortable or safe with a partner, if we feel we can be open and honest with them, then there'll be nothing to feel ashamed about, especially when it comes to saying no. The right person will never make us feel bad about who we are before, during, or after sex. It's just that getting to know someone that well and having those kinds of open and truthful conversations isn't something we're taught as boys. We're told to jump at any opportunity for sex and worry about feelings later. We're told that men act on their sexual impulses without a second thought. This couldn't be further from the truth.

It's not just about understanding when something unexpected happens. When we're comfortable and connected with a partner as a whole person—when we're able to share our thoughts, interests, and desires with someone who we know will appreciate them—we experience sex in a way we couldn't if there wasn't that level of vulnerability, of connection, of intimacy. Sex is meant to be emotional and pleasurable, and it requires vulnerability to get there, and when it happens between people who trust and respect each other, who create a safe space, it's an awesome thing.

That's the big secret, the thing no one will ever learn from mainstream porn. Sex is sharing the most honest and vulnerable parts of ourselves.

While it might make me seem old-fashioned and boring, from everything I know about sex and all my experience, I still believe sex is best reserved for two emotionally mature people in a committed relationship. But that's just my opinion. You might feel or think differently, and that's okay. All I ask is that you respect and appreciate the beauty of sex, not just because it's a natural part of our humanity, but because of the spiritual connection that comes from it when we're intimate with someone we care about.

SEXUAL ASSAULT IS (SADLY) MORE COMMON THAN YOU MIGHT THINK

In so many of our minds, sexual assault might be this horrible thing that happens to other people. It doesn't happen to you, your family, your friends, or your neighbors.

I wish I could tell you that is the case. Unfortunately, it's not. And devastatingly, a lot of us already know this from firsthand experience.

According to the National Sexual Violence Resource Center, 734,630 people were sexually assaulted in America in 2018. Even worse, only 25 percent of them reported it to the police. This means there are most likely people in our lives right now who have been sexually assaulted, but because of how heartbreaking a subject sexual assault is, and how traumatic it can be for survivors to discuss, people often live with sexual assault in silence.

So why do victims keep their trauma inside, you ask? A few reasons, and honestly, a lot of it is because of what happens when they tell the truth. Did you know that out of every 1,000 sexual assaults that happen only 250 are reported to the police?

Read any online post about someone's experience with sexual assault and abuse, and you're pretty much guaranteed to find dozens of comments blaming the victim, trying to poke holes in their story, or siding with the accused. "Why'd you wait so long to come forward?" "Do you have any proof?" "It sounds like the person who assaulted you also helped you a lot." "But you wanted it, too . . . that's not sexual assault." "It sounds like you might have consented." "You should've known better than to let this happen." "You shouldn't have been naked with them then; your actions say you consented." "Do you really want to ruin this person's career/family/life by saying this?"

Imagine that—being sexually assaulted, finally coming

SEXUAL ASSAULT

Think sexual assault is something rare that doesn't happen to most people? Wrong. Someone is sexually assaulted somewhere in America **every 68 seconds**.

The most recent data from RAINN (Rape, Abuse & Incest National Network) also says that:

- One in 9 girls and 1 in 53 boys under the age of eighteen experience sexual abuse or assault at the hands of an adult.
- 82 percent of all victims under 18 are female.
- Young women (ages 16 to 19) are four times more likely than the general population to be victims of sexual assault.

forward about this traumatic thing that has happened to you . . . and having people acting like *you* were to blame.

That's why standing with survivors of sexual assault is so important.

If you are a survivor, know that there are people who will believe you, who will help you get the care you need to be safe and to heal. If a friend or family member tells us about being forced to do something sexually (any form of sexual touch without consent is a violation) by someone else, first know that it took a lot of courage for them to share that with us. We must be a safe person in their life, and that's the kind of person we should all strive to be. We can let them know that we believe them, support them, and that they deserve to be heard and to heal.

It's also important for us to know that this stuff is too heavy to carry alone, in the same way that it's too heavy for the survivor to carry alone. A safe and trusted adult(s) should get involved so that the person can get the help they need. Until then, we might tell that person something like this:

"I'm so sorry this happened, and I believe you. You did not deserve it. I'm glad you felt safe enough to share this with me, but do you feel comfortable talking with an adult that you trust?"

They might tell us that it has to stay a secret and we can't tell anyone. There are secrets that are not safe to keep, and this is one of them.

Even though we (or they) might feel like we're not being a good friend, keeping a secret is never worth the cost of someone's safety. Reaching out to a trusted adult for help is the best thing to do, believe me.

There also might be times when we're in a situation where we can help protect others if an assault is happening or about to happen. If we EVER see someone who appears to be uncomfortable telling another person no (with their words or their body language); if they are under the influence of alcohol or drugs and someone is sexually touching them, we need to immediately step in and say or do something, like call the police. Silence is never the answer when safety is involved. This is what being man enough looks like.

THE NOT-SO-DIRTY TRUTH

This chapter about sex is pretty long compared to some of the other chapters, but it's a complex subject and I really wanted to be honest in a way I wish someone had been with me. What's wild is that there is so much I wasn't able to cover because the publisher told me the book is already too long! Hopefully, as uncomfortable as this might have been, it answered a few questions for you.

Also one of the best things about books is that we can go back and reread them as things come up in our lives, and at least for me as I grow and evolve, my understanding of the text grows and evolves too. So maybe the next time you read this chapter it will hit different and feel like you are reading it for the first time with new eyes.

The main takeaway here is that I don't want you to be afraid or worried about your sexuality and how you express it and experience it. I want you to know you can approach it at your own pace, and in your own time.

Whatever your orientation is, as you navigate the obstacle course of sexuality as a boy, keep your head on straight and your heart involved, and check in with your gut. Do what feels right, and do your best to ignore the messages that say us boys are emotionless, sex-obsessed beasts. Try to remember that while your physical impulses and desires are healthy and natural, they're just one piece of the human experience. There's absolutely nothing wrong with sex, but the best kind of sex is not what's seen in porn. It's 100 percent about being emotionally and spiritually connected while creating a safe space for our partners to do the same. That's where love comes in . . . but that's a whole different chapter.

BREAKING IT DOWN

SEXUALITY COMES IN ALL SHAPES AND SIZES.

Cultural influencers might be saying that you're inherently sexual all the time, but that doesn't have to be true. Each person's sexual experience is their own.

OUR PENISES ARE NOT OUR SEXUAL SELVES.

There's so much more to a boy's sexuality than their penis. Don't feel the need to put all your thoughts and time into worrying about it.

PORN ISN'T SEXUAL EDUCATION.

Pornography doesn't depict sex at its healthiest or most realistic, and you can also become dependent because of how it affects our dopamine pathways.

PHONES AND SOCIAL MEDIA CREATE NEW PRESSURES.

We need to be careful of using our phones for sending, asking for, and receiving sexual pictures. Sharing these pictures can be a violation of consent, and is often harmful, and at times, illegal.

CONSENT IS ALWAYS NEEDED.

It is always necessary to get an enthusiastic yes from a sexual partner. There are no gray areas or exceptions to the rule, and consent can be taken back at any time.

SEXUAL ASSAULT IS MORE COMMON THAN YOU THINK.

Sexual assault is very real and causes deep harm to victims. If you have been abused or assaulted, it is not your fault and you deserve to heal. Healing will take time, and the best thing you can do is find a safe person or place to report it.

SEX IS PART OF CONNECTION.

For all the hype surrounding it, sex is at its best when two emotionally mature people are expressing their deep love and feelings for each other physically. Let's never lose the emotion and humanity behind sexual experiences.

7

BOYS WILL BE KNIGHTS

THE BIG L

Love.

Where do we begin?

What are boys even taught about love growing up?

Where do we learn how to love someone? From our parents? From our friends? From the movies?

The basic idea behind the kind of fairy-tale love we have seen in the movies is that the boy saves the day, right? We kill the dragon, or usher our love interest into a cool car, and everyone lives happily ever after. Our love is a powerful force that gives new purpose to those who get to experience it. Our love is so big, so important, that if we give it to someone, it's going to change everything for them. It's going to save them. (Thank God for *Frozen* and it finally being about the love of two sisters that saves the day.)

But most of the time, the love depicted in films is not real. Take it from a guy who makes movies—very rarely are these stories based in reality, and if they are, 99 percent of the time the stakes have to be raised to entertain an audience because the real love story wasn't quite *enough*. That's right; the real love wasn't enough. Or maybe it was and we have just been conditioned to think that real love is weak and boring.

Regardless, Hollywood love, and even the love you read about in books or hear about in songs, create unfair expectations that, without even realizing it, leave many of us frustrated and angry. Not with the movies and the other media we like, but with the love in our own lives. It makes us worry that if our love doesn't play out like a Hollywood movie, it's flawed, or we got a fake version of it because we don't deserve the real thing. That's like expecting your parents to get you a sports car for Christmas and being disappointed when the Ferrari doesn't show up. The difference is, of course, that love is a lot harder to define than a sports car. And instead of a cool ride on the line, it's your heart.

When it comes to love, there are a lot of questions to unpack. For starters, what does love look like, and how do we recognize it? Can love start as a friendship, or can a friendship even exist without love?

Love is a mystery in many ways, but we do know that love is as varied as the humans on this planet. And as we discussed in the previous chapter, every person is different, and each one of us has deep wells of thought and emotion within us. There are so many types of relationships, so many ways in which people can love each other.

So let's put the fairy tales behind us and shoot a different movie. A messy, uncomfortable, and awesome one.

AND THEN THE MALE OF THE SPECIES DOES A LITTLE DANCE: THE PERFORMANCE OF BOYS' LOVE

Over the past couple of chapters, we've talked about how it's usually girls who have to *do* something to be considered successful or worthwhile. Boys already *are* something—smart, strong, cool—but girls have to work for it. And that's true in love, too, in a lot of ways.

But love is a time in a boy's life in which he is expected

to do something. The problem is, guys often get pressured into focusing on all the wrong things, and then their priorities get thrown out of whack.

So far, the rules of masculinity we've encountered time and time again have been:

- Show no feelings.
- Never let them know you like her, or him, or them.
- Be chill.

Whether we're standing on the edge of a bridge or sharing our heart with someone, boys are supposed to approach everything with total calm, like it's no big deal. So we're taught to act a little distant, not to look desperate, to play it cool when you have a crush. A lot of times we're even told to pretend we don't like the person we're interested in.

Except love is undeniable. It's impossible to "show no feelings," because we're dealing with one of the two all-consuming feelings human beings have ever experienced. So when we fall in love, we either put it on blast or act like we aren't really in love to protect ourselves. Confusing, right?

Now, if we do decide to dive in and go for it, we think it needs to be big. Like we need to declare our love to the entire world so that the person we are in love with can see how lucky they would be to have us. Like we have to win them, beating out other contenders like it's some sort of reality dating competition show (don't even get me started on those). And to be fair, this doesn't just come from men; society has conditioned many women to want and unfortunately expect the fairy tale too.

What's hard is that after being told to act like we don't really care for most of our lives, boys suddenly have to deal with caring about someone more than anything. What's even more bizarre is that sometimes we pretend we care more than we do just to "get" the person. Because getting them must mean we are enough, right? If we can win someone's heart, maybe the fairy tale is true!

See, when it comes to love and dating, it doesn't seem like it's enough to be ourselves. It's almost like we have to express our adoration in the most elaborate way possible. I know this well. I have spent my life being the king of big romantic gestures. You name it, I've probably done it. I even planned what might be one of the world's most elaborate marriage proposals when I made my wife, Emily, a twenty-seven-minute interactive movie that she didn't even know she was in until the end. (It's true, and it's on YouTube.)

But if I really sit with myself and go deep into the real *why* of proposing that way, a part of it was actually because I didn't feel enough. Not just for her, but for everyone. Sure, I'm a filmmaker and a romantic and all that, but one of my dear

> ## "WHERE THERE IS LOVE, NOTHING IS TOO MUCH TROUBLE AND THERE IS ALWAYS TIME."
>
> **◄ 'ABDU'L-BAHÁ ►**

friends, Jay Shetty, once told me that there is no such thing as a completely pure intention. It's only a percentage pure, and our goal should be to have that percentage be as high as possible. So when I think about the deeper reasons for many of the romantic gestures in my life, while some of that percentage was sincere, some also absolutely had to do with impressing Emily and showing the world just how much love I had to give.

Whether it's writing long dramatic letters or asking our crushes to the dance by filling their locker with balloons or flowers, while a lot of it is sweet and innocent and about our feelings, there might be some other more self-centered motivations at play, too.

Nothing says it better than the idea of "winning" someone over.

Let's break this down for a second: What does it mean to "win" when it comes to love? Well, first it means thinking of the person we have feelings for as an object or thing that we have to "get," and, if all works out, "keep." Maybe you noticed that the language I just used was possessive here? I did that on purpose because men speak like this all the time when we talk about relationships, especially heterosexual ones. But let me clear something up: the people we love aren't something to show off in a trophy case or add to a collection. People aren't the "objects of our affection" or the prey we need to hunt. We're all on the same level, looking for the same thing: proof that we're enough.

AFTER THE GRAND GESTURE

Let's say a huge performative gesture works and our love interests return the favor . . . and then we realize that we don't actually *like* them that much. We were attracted to them, yes, and maybe thought we would be great together, but then as soon as they said YES, our interest went away. Well, this can happen because boys and men are often conditioned to be more excited about the thrill of the chase than the actual person we're chasing. I know a lot of guys who fantasize about being with someone until they are actually with them, and suddenly the person they were after isn't worth the effort anymore. And when a boy loses interest after a hot pursuit, the other person is left to do whatever they can to keep the boy's attention.

See, having a crush on someone, or even being in love with them, is way different from *liking* someone. Liking somebody means liking who they are every day. It means enjoying the time you spend together and wanting to get to know more about their life.

The public displays of affection, the big showy gestures—those can be really exciting (one of the reasons why also has to do with dopamine). But knowing that you truly *like* someone beyond all that is where the real excitement is, because you've made a connection that's meaningful, and, best of all, real.

A QUICK REMINDER ABOUT CONSENT

We talked about consent a lot in the last chapter, but it's something to mention here, too, because big performative gestures can cross the line of emotional consent. True, we never get to choose who we fall in love with, but what if the people we love don't want our relationship in the spotlight? What if being on display makes them really, *really* nervous, especially if they're in a position where being open about the relationship might not be 100 percent safe?

By building trust with someone and learning to communicate with them, we learn what their boundaries are. And if we love someone, respecting boundaries is a crucial part of showing them that you respect them.

And truthfully, that respect is extended to the people who don't return our love the way we want them to, although for many of us, that's the hardest fact to accept. Always remember, we want to love someone the way that THEY want to be loved, not the way WE want to love them.

> ## "LOVE IS AN ACTION, NEVER SIMPLY A FEELING."
>
> ### BELL HOOKS

PASSION PLAY: A DEEP BREATH BEFORE CHARGING INTO LOVE

I'm a passionate person, if you couldn't tell already. When I like something, I tend to become fixated on it. Whether it's a new gadget or a sport I've just heard about, I try to learn as much as I can about the things that fascinate me. But that passion can also come across as intensity when it's transferred from a thing or a hobby and onto a person.

For example, when I first met Emily and we'd go to a party, I had no interest in hanging out with anyone else. The only person I wanted to be around was her. I was so happy that regardless of who I was talking to, I'd always look around to see where she was and then find my way over to her. She was new and exciting, and I couldn't get enough of her.

Later, though, I found out that while I thought I was being charming and making her feel special, it was actually having the opposite effect. Emily refers to that as my "little puppy dog phase" (for the record, not what I was going for). It was like if she left my sight, she could feel me searching for her in the crowd. It made her want to hide from me. Sure, puppies are cute, but their need for constant attention can also be super annoying. We don't want to be puppies.

Now, some guys might find this confusing. All I did was show Emily how interested in her I was—and that turned her *off*? The thing is, Emily didn't mind being the subject of my affection, or even my passion. It was just that once the floodgates of my emotions were open, I was hitting her with a tidal wave of feelings, and she felt like she was drowning in them. What I didn't realize at the time is that she needed a break from my passion. Which is only natural, because everything in life needs a pause or a resting period in order to function properly.

Just think about your breath right now. You inhale, pause, and then exhale out. You don't just keep inhaling, right? Now think about your heart. With each beat, it expands and contracts so that our blood can keep pumping. One more example: if we water plants every day, they will die because they also need time to absorb the water. I think of love like this, especially at the beginning of relationships.

Speaking of the beginning of relationships, have you ever heard the word "infatuation"? Infatuation is an intense passion for someone (or something) new. When people are infatuated with each other, it's all rainbows, butterflies, and harps. But infatuation usually doesn't last, because eventually every relationship becomes familiar.

For boys, infatuation can be more complicated or even

intense, because we're taking off our amor and letting our hearts off the leash for maybe the first time. But when the thrill of infatuation wears off, we can be left wondering if we made a mistake because the excitement and big displays have fizzled out. Or maybe we question whether we know how to love at all.

The important thing to remember is that infatuation is a signal that we want to know all we can about the person who interests us. And how do we really get to know someone else?

I believe there's only one real way. The thing is, it's not flashy, or cool, or the kind of thing that will blow up on social media. We can't capture it with a camera, and it's not going to make us popular or help build our social following. The only way to get to know someone is through building a foundation of honesty, communication, and, most of all, trust. And while I am here to tell you that it 100 percent works, the only way it works is if both people are willing to make the effort.

So what if we started right now? What if instead of trying to impress each other with a whirlwind of big gestures and performed love, we all just put our cards on the table and were super honest with each other? What if instead of burying someone under the weight of the emotions we have been holding so close to our hearts for so long, we take it slow and one feeling at a time? What if at the very beginning of the dating process and before the infatuation wears off, we tell each other the things about ourselves that we are insecure about or embarrassed by? I mean, after all, don't we want someone to know who we truly are, not just the parts of us we feel are safe to show?

Think of an essay you've been assigned a month in advance—sure, you can try to write it all in one night, in a massive rush of inspiration, but that usually just ends with you feeling tired the next morning and bummed out later when you get a C-minus (I speak from personal experience). But if you do a little work every night for the whole month, the paper is a lot more solid, and you have time to reread it later and think, *Hmmm, is this what I actually meant?*

Romance and infatuation are fun—there's nothing like watching someone's eyes light up when they see us. But ultimately, we want to be close to and know the people who light us up. In order for that to happen, we must let that person actually see *us* and then create some space so that they can keep seeing us—and hopefully hearing those harps—for a long time.

GUT CHECK

THE EX-CRUSH

Write down the name of someone you had a crush on. Did you truly love them, like *Romeo and Juliet*—style LOVE, or no? Did that crush become a friendship, or even nothing at all? Jot down what happened with this person and why your feelings may have changed.

THE DREADED FRIEND ZONE, AND OTHER MYTHS

Some of you might have read my story about Emily being turned off by my "puppy dog" behavior and thought that she was being unfair. Like she should be happy that I was showing so much interest in her. That my story was proof that guys who are nice or vulnerable aren't appreciated. This is an idea that's rampant right now (especially on the internet) and has been reinforced through the chains of masculinity for years. I think it's something we ought to dive into a little.

Because boys are usually taught to be emotionless, putting our feelings out there is a huge step. Even if a grand gesture is kind of hollow, the very act of admitting that we're interested in someone can sometimes feel like a sacrifice. We've slain the dragon of our own self-consciousness, and now we're here for the reward . . . and if we get rejected, we demand to know why. We've been told that we're *entitled* to that reward. How *dare* they reject the efforts of our love?

Except in this scenario, our reward is a person's love and acceptance—and that person just might not be interested in us. Because, well . . . they're a person, too. Maybe the damsel, whatever gender they may be, isn't a damsel after all. Maybe they don't like the whole "being rescued" thing and would prefer not to be approached that way. Maybe we're just not their type of knight. Or maybe they weren't in peril in the first place. Maybe they had a really nice thing going with the dragon.

All these reasons for someone not reciprocating feelings are totally valid. Is it a bummer? Yes, for sure, and yet . . . it's still valid.

But remember how I said that love was one of the two all-consuming feelings known to humankind? The other one is fear. And sometimes they can seem indistinguishable.

What do I mean by that? Well, in my experience, love makes us vulnerable, and being vulnerable can make us feel afraid, so sometimes the voices in our heads that caution us

> **"I BELIEVE THAT EVERY SINGLE EVENT IN LIFE HAPPENS IN AN OPPORTUNITY TO CHOOSE LOVE OVER FEAR."**
>
> **OPRAH WINFREY**

from doing something or daring us to act can sound exactly the same. When we can't tell if love or fear is influencing our behavior, it leads to great deal of self-doubt. Putting on our armor seems like the only logical thing to do, right? When I freeze up emotionally like that, I try to quiet my mind and be still. I slow down my breath and let myself feel whatever feelings come up in that moment. When I do that, love always finds a way to overcome fear, and I'm reminded that a choice rooted in love will always be more powerful and work out better in the long run than a choice rooted in fear.

Okay, back to the knight! His whole life, the knight

has been taught that if he goes on the quest and fights the dragon (puts himself out there, admits he has feelings), then he deserves something in return. But when a damsel rejects him, he gets scared. What if he's not so strong and brave and worthy after all? What if the rules he's been taught his whole life, that doing his best will get him whatever he wants, are being broken? What if the rules are fake?

Instead of being scared, the knight tries to find another way out. It can't be something wrong with *him* or his actions, or with the way things are, because those have worked out for him pretty well so far.

There must be something wrong with the damsel. Maybe they're too dumb to realize what they had. What an idiot! Well, he was too good for them anyway!

This is a display of male privilege that's frighteningly common—the feeling that if we play by the so-called rules, we are entitled to whatever or whomever we want. It's even become a cliché on the internet: the *Nice Guy*. How often have we heard of this idea of the Nice Guy always finishing last? Like the myth of the alpha wolf, it's just a bunch of BS. Nice Guys are not the poor victim in a massive global plot against them. They're just trying to deflect their feelings of disappointment and hurt onto the person who "rejected" them.

INTERPRETING YOUR FEAR

Have you ever experienced the feelings of fear and love at the same time? Like asking someone to a dance, or trying out for a sports team or the school play? Fear shows up in all areas of our lives as biological messaging meant to protect us. But fear can also be a powerful tool of personal insight. How does your fear show up? When do you feel afraid?

Take a moment right now and try to slow down your breathing. Close your eyes and think of something you are afraid of. What sensations can you feel in your body right now? Do your hands get sweaty? Is your heart beating faster or stronger? Do you feel something in the pit of your stomach? Sit with that for a moment. Now ask yourself: What is your fear trying to tell you? That you care? That you need a break, or better support and boundaries? Do you need to ask for help? Explore whatever came up for you by writing it down in a journal or talking about it with someone you trust.

Think of it this way: Nice Guy (that's his name) was "one of the good ones." He was really sweet to his crush.

He helped them with their homework, went out of his way for them, brought them gifts, the whole nine yards . . . but then that person either dumped him, or dated someone else! In Nice Guy's mind, it can't be that *he* did something wrong, because he was so *nice*. It must mean that people are only interested in dating jerks. They must crave the drama of loving someone who doesn't return their love. Someone who is emotionally unavailable. Someone uncertain. But is this really true, or is this a story he's telling himself because he's feeling insecure? Either way, if Nice Guy reacts out of a place of victimhood, frustration, or anger at why he wasn't chosen, it just shows he wasn't nice after all.

A byproduct of Nice Guys blaming others for their misfortunes is an idea called "the friend zone." The concept is that if we're *too* nice to someone, become *too* friendly with them, or get too vulnerable they'll stick us in the friend zone and therefore never consider us a romantic or sexual possibility. They'll love us *like a brother*. And then we're stuck pining for this person, totally in love with them, while they go on to date guys who we don't think are right for them or who treat them like crap.

So first, let's just call it:

There's no such thing as the friend zone. There's just love and friendship. Sorry, guys.

What either is built on is up to us. But I can assure you of one thing: we can't build a friendship without love, and we can't build love without friendship. Yet to make ourselves feel better about not having our love reciprocated, we often take this all-or-nothing stance. But every time we do that, we are cheating ourselves out of connections with people who enrich our lives in ways we never could have imagined.

> ## "THE BEST AND MOST BEAUTIFUL THINGS IN THE WORLD CANNOT BE SEEN OR EVEN TOUCHED— THEY MUST BE FELT WITH THE HEART."
>
> **HELEN KELLER**

Honestly, as a straight guy, I'd be lost without my female friends. Some of us have known each other for twenty years, and thankfully there have never been any complicated romantic feelings between us. They've been there for me when I was at my lowest, celebrated with me when my dreams started coming true, and pushed me to be a better person. I've done the same in return, too. It's hard to think about giving all that up because our culture doesn't value the friendships of straight men and women at all—and the sad fact is, there's a lot of dudes out there who just see those friendships as an opportunity.

Here's an example: some boys will pretend to be a girl's friend to get into her inner circle and then try to change the nature of the relationship. When that happens, the friendship quickly becomes unsafe for her because she can tell there is an ulterior motive, and the trust she once had is now shaken. This happens in relationships of all kinds, between all genders, too. No matter who is involved, friendships need to be safe spaces, and it's our responsibility as boys to keep them safe, because for so long, boys and men have abused their power and privilege when they didn't get what they wanted. (More on that in a bit.)

So, with all that said: What do we do when we have romantic feelings for someone who clearly just wants to be friends with us?

Well, maybe it's best to accept that those feelings of love make for the roots of a really good friendship. We can be attracted to someone, physically and/or emotionally, but be much more compatible as friends because our personalities match up that way. Also, those feelings of attraction don't always (or even most of the time) have to be acted on. While our feelings might be strong, what matters most is what we do with those feelings, and in some situations, doing nothing is the best thing to do. That might sound backward, but it's true! For example, we're going to be attracted to a lot of people over the course of our lives. We will still be attracted to people while we're in a committed relationship and even a marriage, but that doesn't mean we should act on those feelings and betray another person's trust. So why can't we respect our friendships enough to hold back?

And when it comes to a "friends with benefits" type of relationship (where you have sex but no romantic or emotional connection to each other), that can go south pretty quickly and mess up a friendship that could have lasted a lifetime. Let's face it: while plenty of crushes and relationships bloom swiftly and then wilt like flowers, friendships are often lasting and sturdy like redwoods.

But what if we go for it, tell someone how we feel, and we start to date, and then it doesn't work out? Well, guess what? Rock-solid friendships can also form after a breakup, too. Some people are even best friends with their exes. Breakups aren't always these giant missiles that leave huge craters; sometimes they're just leaves turning orange and blowing off a tree. (And now I'm suddenly craving a pumpkin spice latte, and I don't even like them.)

Anyway, the point I'm trying to make is if you buy into this friend zone concept and get bent out of shape when someone you like offers you their hand but not their heart, maybe you need to take a second and self-reflect on why you feel the need to slap their hand away.

Hold on, that's harsh. I'm not pointing fingers, saying you, yes, *YOU*, Larry Teasdale from Lincoln, Nebraska, need to check yourself. (PS—If you're a kid from Lincoln, Nebraska, named Larry Teasdale, I'm sorry to have called you out. I swear, I just came up with two names and a city. It's nothing personal. You're a good kid, Larry. Thanks for reading my book.)

Okay, now here's the *really* harsh part. Apologies ahead of time.

Let's say, for the sake of argument, that there *is* a friend zone. Let's say some people will put us in a mental box they have set aside for big brothers and nice dogs and other things they find cute but aren't attracted to.

The answer to that is: So what?! Not everyone is going to like us, and we shouldn't be trying to convince or manipulate someone into liking us either. Also, the last thing we should ever do is then try to change ourselves so another person can like us. It never works because that person isn't really liking us at all. They are liking whatever personality we are faking. If someone doesn't like us it just means that this person is not our person, and it's time to let it go. Not just for them, but for us!

And here's another thought: Maybe they do like you! Just *not in that way*. As much of a downer as that is, it's going to happen.

This is hard for me to tell you, because deep down I love that romantic idea that being a good dude gets the universe's attention and earns you a reward. That'd be really nice. But that's just not true, especially with love. Sometimes, we might work *really* hard to make people like us, but it's just not going to happen.

Why? Well, there are probably a billion reasons, and most of them have nothing to do with us. Maybe there's a lack of compatibility, chemistry, and physical attraction. Maybe there are certain things about us that remind them of someone who broke their trust. Again, we have no control over any of that. And when all is said and done, we should remember that even famous athletes, movie stars, and world-leaders have been heartbroken because they weren't a good match for someone else.

We've covered a lot of ground so far, but here are the things I want you to remember: there is more to life than romantic relationships, and we NEED friends like we need air to breathe. If we like someone who doesn't like us back in a romantic way, if we are willing to accept it, we still get to have that awesome person in our lives. And who knows, if we can truly learn to be happy for someone else and be a friend to them, we may be surprised if one day it comes back around.

But that can only happen if we choose to let our feelings go.

> # "YOUR TASK IS NOT TO SEEK FOR LOVE, BUT MERELY TO SEEK AND FIND ALL THE BARRIERS WITHIN YOURSELF THAT YOU HAVE BUILT AGAINST IT."
>
>  **RUMI**
> **THIRTEENTH-CENTURY PERSIAN POET**

HULKING OUT: DEALING WITH REJECTION

One time, I was having dinner with a friend of mine and she was telling me about an awful date she'd gone on. The guy was pushy, loud, and mean to their waiter. I thought it was strange that she even went out with him in the first place, so I asked her why she did. When I heard her answer, it floored me.

"I was honestly worried about what he'd do if I said no."

Boys and men are taught to be so emotionally impenetrable that when we put our hearts on the line, we can become dangerously fragile if someone we like is disinterested in us. And unfortunately, guys who get rejected by their crushes often behave poorly. We lash out, say terrible things, spread awful stories, and cast the person who rejected us as our enemy. We're raised to be so obsessed with being tough and impossible to hurt that when we feel humiliated or embarrassed, we tend to hurt back just so that we can regain some power.

And in the back of our minds, we think it's okay because we're men. If there's one emotion that the messages of masculinity give men permission to feel, it's anger.

Breakups can definitely be a real "boys will be boys" moment, where everyone accepts a man's anger because he's so devastated. But we've got to stop normalizing this, because it's not a good look for anyone. I mean there's even a category of porn called "revenge porn," where people post naked pictures and videos of their exes to get back at them. (It's a huge betrayal—and illegal.) Getting a pass to act horribly because we don't know how to process our emotions is nothing to be proud of.

So how do we deal with these feelings of bitterness when we're hurt? Well, I can at least tell you what helps me—slowing myself down and being still. By sitting in the pain, sadness, frustration, and anger and allowing myself to actually feel all of it, I can let it go. Running away or being aggressive won't fix anything.

The only way out of it is through it.

Another thing that's helped me in these tough moments is my faith. When I've been overwhelmed with anger and rejection, leaning on my faith has allowed me to look inward and discover why I'm really angry. Maybe I'm actually feeling insecure or sad, and since those feelings are so uncomfortable, I use anger to push them away. But no matter what your religious beliefs are (or even if you don't believe in a higher power), just by letting yourself feel fear and vulnerability, you'll be able move past them—and even learn from them.

By the way, anger is a completely valid emotion. It can

warn us when a boundary has been crossed and teach us a lot about ourselves. It only becomes a problem when we hold on to that feeling for too long. Think of it this way. If anger was a rest stop on the freeway, we might want to stop and grab some fast food and Starbucks, but we wouldn't necessarily want to live there. And if you go deep enough and let yourself feel it, oftentimes just below anger is another feeling: sadness.

Heartbreak is real, but it doesn't have to destroy us or our self-worth. Though it might feel like someone we care about is telling us that we're not enough for them, the disappointment of rejection is also a healthy, necessary way of growing as a person. We need to experience heartbreak to fully appreciate love and become the kindest, most compassionate, loving, open people we can be. Trying to avoid heartache is like going to the gym and not working out because we don't want to feel the burn that makes our muscles grow. Don't be that person who's on their phone the whole time instead of running on the treadmill! FEEL THE BURN and let it strengthen and guide you.

Anyway, if you love the one person who really matters, then everything will end up okay.

And guess who that person is?

I'm kidding! That would be a weird place to take this book, right? It turns out no one can save you but me, Justin Baldoni! My jokes are getting really bad. I think it's time to wrap this up.

Loving *ourselves* is the most important thing we can do.

> ## "I DON'T TRUST PEOPLE WHO DON'T LOVE THEMSELVES AND TELL ME, 'I LOVE YOU' ... THERE IS AN AFRICAN SAYING WHICH IS: BE CAREFUL WHEN A NAKED PERSON OFFERS YOU A SHIRT."
>
> ### MAYA ANGELOU

But sometimes it's also the most difficult thing, because there's a major roadblock in the way: negative self-talk.

Did you know that the average person has over six thousand thoughts per day? Did you also know that the majority of those thoughts are negative ones about ourselves? Yep, it's true.

In my faith, 'Abdu'l-Bahá says that "the reality of man is his thought." So if all we do is judge and think badly about ourselves, we'll believe those thoughts and act as if they're true.

I'm here to tell you, without a doubt, changing those negative thoughts is the key to loving who we are.

Instead of telling ourselves we're weak, we should believe we're courageous.

Instead of telling ourselves we're not smart, we should believe we're intelligent.

Instead of telling ourselves that our bodies aren't perfect, we should believe they're beautiful just as they are.

You get the picture.

So, let's start being kind to ourselves. Often, we're kinder to other people than we are to ourselves, which doesn't make much sense when you think about it. Once we flip the script in our minds and trust that everything inside of us is good, worthy, and enough, we'll be less afraid of love, loss, and anything else that might come our way, and the kinder we will be to others. And the irony of all of it is that the more we love ourselves, the easier we will be to love.

THE LAST WORD ON LOVE

When we act out of love, we show our hearts—and that can make us feel very vulnerable. But vulnerability isn't something we should fear, even though it can be scary.

Showing our hearts means showing our *humanity*. It means embracing and accepting all the emotions we feel instead of being ashamed of them. It also means giving other people space to be vulnerable with us and making them feel safe and accepted.

Showing our hearts does not make us any less of a man. In fact, it makes us more than a man. It makes us *human*.

BREAKING IT DOWN

LOVE IS MORE COMPLICATED THAN ANY FAIRY TALE.

Love is an intense emotion, and experiencing it for the first time can be overwhelming, so try not to rush anything. Also, no one needs to be saved if love is real.

BIG ROMANTIC GESTURES ONLY GO SO FAR.

Expressing feelings for someone in smaller, more practical ways is just as meaningful as big public displays—especially since once the performance is over, many boys often realize that the chase was more important to them.

LOVE IS IMPORTANT IN FRIENDSHIP.

Sometimes the people we are interested in romantically are meant to become our friends. And that's okay. The trust and compassion that comes with love is the foundation of friendships that can change your life for the better.

WE SHOULD NOT PUNISH OTHERS FOR NOT LOVING US BACK.

It's been normalized that boys and men lash out in unhealthy ways when they're romantically rejected. That has to change, so don't let rejection make you act in ways that are hurtful and harmful to others, and to yourself.

BE KIND TO AND *LOVE YOURSELF.*

Negative self-talk gets in the way of us loving and accepting who we are. If we fix that, we can show our hearts and humanity to others without being afraid and finally become not just the *men* we are supposed to be, but the *humans* we are destined to be.

8

BOYS WILL BE
HUMAN

Congratulations! You have reached the final chapter. Wow, I'm getting a little misty-eyed thinking about the nearly 300-page journey we have just gone on together. I am grateful you have made it this far and given me so much of your time. Actually, there really is nothing more valuable on earth than time—so thank you.

There is so much more I wish we could talk about, as these topics are complicated and nuanced. We have covered a lot and yet I feel like we have just scratched the surface! But before we finish, let's go over a few things.

Over the course of this book, we've examined our lives pretty deeply. We've looked at our relationship with our friends, families, teachers, sexuality, even our relationship with the world via privilege. And we've looked at our relationship with ourselves—our bodies, our gut, our head, and our heart.

We've also asked ourselves a lot of questions.

Am I *brave* enough to be *vulnerable?*

Am I *confident* enough to *listen?*

Am I *strong* enough to be *sensitive?*

Now that we've reached the end, we're going to do the least masculine thing that most men can think of. The thing we've been told that men, *real* men, never do.

Surrender.

Wave the white flag.

Not because we've lost. Not because we've been beaten by life or the world. But because it's time to stop playing the game by a set of rules that keeps everyone from winning. We need to accept who we are and who we always have been: Human. Feeling. Thinking. Allowed to love whoever we want. Allowed to love ourselves.

For as long as we can remember, we've been taught never to quit, to fight for what we want, for what we believe in. That second place was the first loser. Winners never quit! If you don't fight for something, was it even worth it? What's an accomplishment if you can't count the scars it left on you, physically, mentally, and emotionally?

But guys, this isn't a fight we'll ever win. Trying to be something bigger, better, or more than a human being with real human emotions is a boxing match with infinite rounds. We're fighting our own better nature, and either the match goes on forever or we beat it unconscious. Maybe it's better if we throw off our gloves and just walk away from the fight. Who says we need to fight anyway? There are better solutions that don't leave one of us beaten and bruised.

In this match, the only person we're fighting is ourselves.

EVERY NEW DAY, MORE ARMOR

We've talked about the rules, assumptions, and barriers we put up as boys as though they're a suit of armor. The goal is, of course, to shed the armor and greet the world vulnerable and unafraid. But sometimes, the armor grows back when the going gets tough. More commonly, though, we put it back on when we feel unsafe and hope no one notices. We tell ourselves we're all better, and then go days and months with the armor still on. Sometimes it's the full suit; other times it's just the helmet or the chest plate.

Why? Well, because life is tough! No matter how ready

> ## "WHEN WE CHOOSE TO STRESS OVER THINGS THAT ARE INSIGNIFICANT, WE LOSE SIGHT OF THE THINGS THAT REALLY MAKE US HAPPY. HAPPINESS IS NOT A LIMITED RESOURCE."
>
> ### ▶ CHRISTOPHER AIFF ◀

we are for the world, at some point it's going to break our hearts, or hurt our feelings, or even just exhaust us. When this happens, it's easy to slip our armor back on, because then we don't have to worry about getting hurt.

But then all we're doing is putting up a barrier between us and the world. We are numbing ourselves by not letting the full beautiful experience of being human touch us in the way it was designed to. By trying to avoid the pain, we are

REACHING FOR ARMOR

Now that you've thought about the emotional armor you wear to make yourself feel safe, write down the times when you've put the armor back on. Then stop and think about why you felt you needed to. What steps can you take to feel secure enough to remove it again?

putting on armor that not only protects us temporarily from feeling the uncomfortable things, but also the good things!

The reason life is beautiful isn't just because of all the good; it's because of all the sadness, frustration, happiness, and joy that exist together. We need the full spectrum of experiences to be able to appreciate them each on their own. If there were no darkness, how would we appreciate the light? If there was no winter, spring would be meaningless. We need the diversity of experiences and feelings to be fully human; otherwise we are just robots.

So watch how you move through the world. Hopefully, you can notice it more now. When you've removed a piece of your internal armor, take a moment to feel how freeing

SELF CARE 101

Becoming a better man is an ongoing, sometimes challenging process. Which is why we should be kind to ourselves, every day. Here are some things you can do to take care of YOU:

- Find a spiritual practice, or, at the very least, believe in something greater than yourself.
- Meditate. Even for five minutes once a day.
- When you feel overwhelmed, practice taking five slow, deep breaths.
- Drink lots of water and move your body. Both can really improve your mood.
- Unplug for a while. Go for a walk without your phone. Notice the world around you.
- Stay connected. Make an effort to check in with the people you care about.
- Be grateful. Think about what made you happy today. Write it down if you can.
- If all else fails, just say to yourself "I am enough."

it is—and when you slip it back on, notice that, too. Being aware is always the first step.

This is the only way we grow. "No pain no gain" isn't

about forcing yourself to fight harder and work faster; it's about being able to withstand the punches life throws at us without falling apart. It's a metaphor not only for physical muscle building, but for emotional and spiritual muscle building, too. If you really think about it, nothing in life grows without a little bit of pain or discomfort. *Nothing.*

All this takes time. It's really difficult. But it's worth it.

And now that we've made it this far, we know we don't have to do it on our own.

NO CLUBS, JUST BOYS

As we have talked about, one of the more harmful myths of masculinity is that we have to do it alone. We need to be the Lone Ranger, the superhero, the *alpha.* The man who has it all together and doesn't need anyone else.

But guess what? We need other people. And they need us. As Bahá'u'lláh says, we "are the fruits of one tree and the leaves of one branch." We are all connected in more ways than we could ever realize. We all need to hear about each other's stories, experiences, feelings. We need to know that while this is our personal journey, it's also a communal one—that there are billions of people out there, all trying to figure it out, all doing their best, all fighting for the greater good.

Let's share our experiences, as humans, from an honest and vulnerable place. Then we can send the elevator back down so that generation after generation can improve and stop repeating the same mistakes. Instead of every man for himself, and the boys' club being somewhere we have to earn entry into, let's open ourselves up to a new world. A world where learning, questioning, curiosity, and growth are the norm. Where everyone is welcome. Where our differences aren't shamed but celebrated. And where we finally realize our full potential as one human family.

"But I can't do that," you might say, "I'm just a kid. And if what I've felt reading this book is true, I might have a lot of problems!"

First of all, if you feel anything like that, just know that you are loved. How do I know? Because I love you. See, love isn't earned, my friend. It's innate. It's already in you and you are already loved because you are alive. You were created with love, and you are love. You are so much more than you could ever realize.

The way you start breaking this cycle and changing things for the future is finding that good within yourself, that part of you that you have maybe up until now kept hidden for self-preservation. A part of you that you can now be proud of because it's what makes you and me and all of us human.

ARE WE DONE YET?

You might be wondering—Where does it end? When do we become "good" men? Is this going to be something we work on our whole lives? Are we ever going to be perfect?

Hate to be a bummer, but:

Yes. We are going to be working on this our entire lives.

And we will never be *perfect* in someone else's eyes.

"Perfect." I don't think I've ever liked that word. But "imperfect"—now, that's a word I've always connected to. Maybe it's because for so long I felt like I was not enough, and creating a goal of imperfection became a way for me to cope with, and accept, my own flaws. Or maybe it was the realization that:

We are and we **will forever be *imperfect.***

True perfection is unattainable, and as a believer in God, a higher power, the universe, I believe that perfection ironically exists in the imperfections. But then one night I realized what I had missed had always been there from the start, and all I had to do was look at the word.

Imperfect = I'm perfect.

Don't you see? Being imperfect is the very thing that makes us perfect. But so many of us feel like we're not good enough because of our imperfections. Maybe it's time we rethink what being enough even means.

We need to try. We *have* to try because:

Enough is enough.

THE BIG TAKEAWAY

This book was never about what's wrong with boys, or what's wrong with boys *being* boys. It's about being true to yourself and understanding that being a boy doesn't require you to behave in certain ways or BE ANYTHING EXCEPT YOURSELF. We aren't redefining masculinity; we're *undefining* it, remember?

Whatever's next, well, that's up to you. But hopefully, after reading this, you know that you are enough, and that is the foundation to being:

Brave enough to apologize when you've done something you know is wrong.

Smart enough to admit you don't know everything and listen to those who know more.

Cool enough to be kind to those who feel alone and also to ourselves.

Big enough to look in the mirror and love your body.

Aware enough to realize that not everyone has the same privileges and experiences and that we must use whatever privilege we have to help those without it.

Man enough to understand consent and view people as people, not objects.

Caring enough to feel whatever feelings need to be felt, even when our hearts are broken.

Loving enough to have compassion for ourselves and the people around us.

Enough, through and through.

Things will change. We will change. The road will veer wildly and wind off into dark woods. But the only thing universal about the journey from our heads to our hearts is that we are worthy enough to take it.

You got this, my friend. I feel like we have earned that title now. You are seen.

You are worthy.

You are loved.

You, my friend, are undoubtedly, 1,000 percent . . . ENOUGH.

ACKNOWLEDGMENTS

Mom and Dad (Sharon and Sam Baldoni), thank you for loving me unconditionally and giving me the freedom to feel. I am so grateful for how supportive you have always been of whatever path I take. This book would never exist without your love, unfailing belief in me, and support of my healing journey. I love you both so much. Emily Baldoni: "If I love you, I need not continually speak of my love— you will know without any words" —'Abdu'l-Bahá. My love, my gratitude for you is endless. You are my helpmate, soul mate, and my partner . . . in all the worlds of God. This book never would have happened without the invisible work that you generously gave behind the scenes. You are magical. Aunt Susie (Shyman), you are the kindest aunt I could have ever asked for. Thank you for being there for me from day one. I love you and Uncle Jim so much.

Noelle René, thank you for always asking me to dig deeper and challenge the status quo. I'm so grateful for your sensitivity, empathy, and superhuman compassion. Johanna Castillo, you are a force of nature, and I am with you until the end. Thank you for pushing me to write this. I needed it just as much as the boys I wrote it for. This doesn't exist without you. Claudia Gabel, your patience, grace, and optimism is second to none. I threw you so many curveballs during the writing of this book and you handled each of them with so much kindness. I can't imagine a better editor for this book, and I can never thank you enough for your support. Chris Krovatin, thank you for helping me turn this idea into a reality and find my older brother voice. I so appreciate you! Jay Roeder, thanks for an amazing cover illustration. It's a knockout.

Claudia V, thank you for giving me the tools to become a safe space, not just for others but for myself. I pray the lessons you have taught me are woven into these pages and the hearts of whoever needs them. Jamey Heath, I love you endlessly, and I hate that I do. Your friendship makes me a better man. Liz Plank, sharing space with you has been such a gift. Your words, insight, and lived experience have made a profound impact on my life. Thank you for loving me and men so much.

Samantha Emmer-Fink, thank you for all you do that no one will ever see. Also, please start wearing a T-shirt on Fridays that says "Don't bother with small talk." Will Youngblood, your support and belief in me has kept me going when I wanted to give up. You mean the world to me, and I will never forget the time, love, and sacrifice you gave me and my family. Brandy Cole, you saved the day (like you always do) with the interior art for this book. Thank you for helping me bring this vision to life. Jen Abel, Matt Mitchell, Stephanie Baum, and the team at JONESWORKS, I so appreciate all the work you've put into to making sure as many boys hear about this book as possible. Thank you for helping spread this message far and wide.

Thanks so much to Suzanne Murphy, Erica Sussman, Cindy Hamilton, Anna Bernard, Robby Imfeld, Patty Rosati, Corina Lupp, Alison Klapthor, Gwen Morton, Rye White, Josh Weiss, Sophie Schmidt, and the entire dream team at HarperCollins for believing in *Boys Will Be Human*. It is a great honor to work with all of you.

SOURCES

INTRODUCTION
Zakrzewski, Vicki. "Debunking the Myths about Boys and Emotions." *Greater Good Magazine*, December 1, 2014, https://greatergood .berkeley.edu/article/item/debunking_myths_boys_emotions.

CHAPTER 2: BOYS WILL BE SMART
"Book Smarts vs. People Smarts: New Study Reveals Why EQ May Matter More Than IQ." PR Web, April 28, 2018, www.prweb.com /releases/2018/04/prweb15443780.htm.

CHAPTER 3: BOYS WILL BE COOL
Caleb, Warren, Todd Pezzuti, and Shruti Koley. "Is Being Emotionally Inexpressive Cool?" *Journal of Consumer Psychology*, February 24, 2018, https://doi.org/10.1002/jcpy.1039.

Miller, Caroline. "Does Social Media Use Cause Depression?: How Heavy Instagram And Facebook Use May Be Affecting Kids Negatively." Child Mind Institute, https://childmind.org/article/is-social-media -use-causing-depression.

National Center for Injury Prevention and Control (U.S.), Division of Violence Prevention. "The Relationship between Bullying and Suicide: What We Know and What It Means for Schools." Centers for Disease Control and Prevention, April 2014. https://stacks.cdc.gov/view/ cdc/34163.

CHAPTER 4: BOYS WILL BE BIGGER
"Study: 94% of Teenage Girls Have Been Body Shamed." WCNC Charlotte, May 2, 2017, www.wcnc.com/article/news/features/study-94-of-teenage -girls-have-been-body-shamed/436143277.

Calzo, Jerel P. et al. "Patterns of Body Image Concerns and Disordered Weight- and Shape-Related Behaviors in Heterosexual and Sexual Minority Adolescent Males." *Developmental Psychology*, September 2015, doi:10.1037/dev0000027.

Kearney–Cooke, Ann, and Diana Tieger. "Body Image Disturbance and the Development of Eating Disorders," in *The Wiley Handbook of Eating Disorders*. West Sussex, UK: Wiley, 2015.

CHAPTER 5: BOYS WILL BE BOYS

Gleig, Ann. "Waking Up to Whiteness and White Privilege." *UCF Today*, October 7, 2020, www.ucf.edu/news/waking-up-to-whiteness-and-white-privilege.

"How Often Are Women Interrupted by Men? Here's What the Research Says." Advisory Board, October 30, 2018, www.advisory.com/Daily-Briefing/2017/07/07/men-interrupting-women.

May, Gareth. "Is the 'Manspreading' Campaign Just Prejudice Against Big Guys?" *The Telegraph*, January 30, 2015, www.telegraph.co.uk/men/thinking-man/11374213/Is-the-manspreading-campaign-just-prejudice-against-big-guys.html.

CHAPTER 7: BOYS WILL BE KNIGHTS

"Do Men Think About Sex Every Seven Seconds?" Snopes, April 18, 2002, www.snopes.com/fact-check/thinking-about-sex.

"LGBT Youth." CDC, www.cdc.gov/lgbthealth/youth.htm.

Herek, Gregory M. "Hating Gays: An Overview of Scientific Studies." *Frontline*, "Assault on Gay America," 2000, www.pbs.org/wgbh/pages/frontline/shows/assault/roots/overview.html.

Mandal, Ananya. "What Is Dopamine?" News Medical, April 9, 2019, www.news-medical.net/health/What-is-Dopamine.aspx.

"Watching Pornography Rewires the Brain to a More Juvenile State." Neuroscience News, December 29, 2019, https://neurosciencenews.com/neuroscience-pornography-brain-15354.

"Statistics." National Sexual Violence Resource Center, www.nsvrc.org/statistics.

"Victims of Sexual Violence: Statistics." RAINN (Rape, Abuse & Incest National Network), www.rainn.org/statistics/victims-sexual-violence.

CHAPTER 8: BOYS WILL BE HUMAN

Murdock, Jason. "Humans Have More Than 6,000 Thoughts per Day, Psychologists Discover." *Newsweek*, July 15, 2020, www.newsweek.com/humans-6000-thoughts-every-day-1517963.

FURTHER READING

Acho, Emmanuel. *Uncomfortable Conversations with a Black Boy*. New York: Roaring Brook Press, 2021.

Brooks, Ben. *Stories for Boys Who Dare to Be Different: True Tales of Amazing Boys Who Changed the World without Killing Dragons*. New York: Running Press Kids, 2018.

Bunch, Ted, and Anna Marie Johnson Teague. *The Book of Dares: 100 Ways for Boys to Be Kind, Bold, and Brave*. New York: Random House Children's Books, 2021.

Chopra, Deepak. *Teens Ask Deepak: All the Right Questions*. New York: Simon Pulse, 2006.

Robarts, Adam J. T., and Lou Aronica. *Nineteen: 19 Insights Learned from a 19-year-old with Cancer*. New York: Regan Arts, 2022.

Todnem, Scott. *Growing Up Great!: The Ultimate Puberty Book for Boys*. California: Rockridge Press, 2019.

ABOUT THE AUTHOR

Justin Baldoni has many roles in his life—actor, director, producer, entrepreneur, philanthropist—but the most important to him are all behind the scenes: his role as a Bahá'í in service to humankind, a husband to his wife Emily, and a father to his kids, Maiya and Maxwell. Justin values service, sincerity, and vulnerability. Through Wayfarer Studios, a film and television studio that he co-founded, he creates art and entertainment that inspires, connects, and unites people. Over the past ten years he has been on a personal journey to figure out what it means for him to be a man— what it means to be a human—in the world today. He has spoken about this journey in his popular TED Talk, on college campuses across America, and on *The Man Enough Podcast*, which he co-hosts.